Dedicated to the memory of
Larry Griffin

'O'Drisceoil's  ... ar narrative and
lavish and haunting ... ...ay become the definitive
statement on Larry ...'

The Irish Times

'O'Drisceoil paints a vivid picture that is not just exacting in
its reconstruction of events, but also fleshes out the human
tragedy.'

RTÉ Guide

'... lifts the lid on an incredibly complex culture of lies,
conspiracy and intimidation that prevented justice being done.'

The Mayo News

'... a tremendous insight into an extraordinary historical event,
brilliantly written ...'

Niall O'Dowd, The Irish Voice

Fachtna Ó Drisceoil

THE
MISSING
POSTMAN

What really happened to Larry Griffin?

MERCIER PRESS

IRISH PUBLISHER – IRISH STORY

MERCIER PRESS

Cork

www.mercierpress.ie

© Fachtna Ó Drisceoil, 2011

ISBN: 978 1 85635 693 0

10 9 8 7 6 5 4 3

A CIP record for this title is available from the British Library

Printed and bound in the EU.

Contents

Acknowledgements

I wish to thank the relatives of Larry Griffin for trusting me to do justice to his story, especially Larry's daughter-in-law Bridie Griffin and his grandchildren Willie Griffin, Leo Griffin, Marian Kilmartin, Seamus Mulrennan and Marie Finnerty.

I also acknowledge the following contributions to this book: my RTÉ colleague Garry Mac Donncha first suggested the story of the missing postman as an idea for a television programme; Kevin Cummins produced and directed the *CSÍ* programme on the missing postman; researcher Margaret Martin got hold of important witness statements; Dr Tadhg Ó Dúshláine of Roinn na Gaeilge, NUI Maynooth, generously gave me a copy of his unpublished manuscript of folklore and information about the case of the missing postman; Seán and Síle Murphy of Kilmacthomas provided help and encouragement for this project from the start; Colum Cronin made enquiries for me in West Cork; Joe Quelly made enquiries for me in County Clare; Jack Burchaell made enquiries for me in County Waterford; Shem Kennedy gave feedback on drafts of the book, helped with research and drew the maps for the book; Sinéad Crowley, Anna

Heussaff, Séamus Ó Drisceoil and Treasa Harkin read drafts of the book and gave invaluable feedback; Gerard Lovett (general secretary of the Garda Síochána Retired Members Association) helped me access information and photographs; Sonny Ward and John Harold provided information and photographs relating to ex-Garda William Murphy; Pauline Clifford (daughter of Garda John Sullivan) shared information and photographs; Seamus O'Brien (former postman in Kilmacthomas) shared his memories with me; Maureen Doherty (daughter of Superintendent James Hunt) gave me a photograph of her father.

I acknowledge the assistance of the staff of the Garda Museum and Archives – the former curator Inspector Pat McGee, the current curator Sergeant Paul Malone and Gerry Kilgannon. I also acknowledge the assistance of Michael Talty and Lara Harte of the RTÉ reference library, the staff of the National Library and the staff of the National Archives.

I wish to thank the Mercier Press team for their encouragement and support.

I also wish to thank all those who helped me but did not wish their names to be mentioned here, and anyone I have inadvertently omitted to mention.

Thanks to Eugenie Regan and Stephen McCormack of Stradbally for their hospitality.

Thanks to my son Mac Dara who provided me with the motivation to finish this book before the deadline of his expected birth in August 2010!

Above all, however, I wish to thank my wife Mary for her love, support and encouragement. *Is tusa mo ghrá geal.*

A NOTE ON DIALOGUE

With the following exceptions all the quotations and reported speech in this book are taken directly from garda documents, newspapers and other sources:

1. the greeting shouted by a passer-by to Larry Griffin in Chapter 1;
2. the conversation between Larry and his family in Chapter 1. This conversation is based on accounts given later by Larry's family;
3. the conversation between Larry and his next-door neighbours in Chapter 2. Larry did visit his neighbours that morning to give presents to the children;
4. the dialogue between Mike and Danny Murphy and their father Jamsie at the start of Chapter 21. This is based on the account given by Mike Murphy to his son Seán.

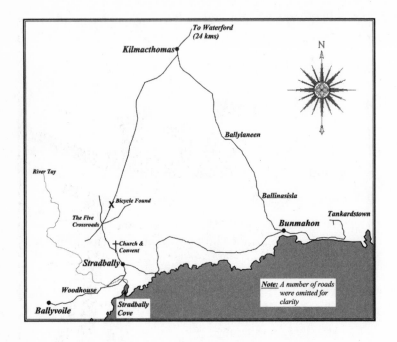

MAP OF THE STRADBALLY AREA

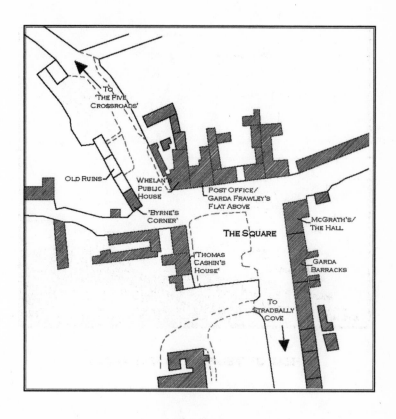

MAP OF STRADBALLY VILLAGE

Main characters

Larry Griffin – the missing postman

Mary Griffin – Larry's wife

Sergeant James Cullinane – sergeant of Stradbally garda barracks

Garda Edward (Ned) Dullea – Stradbally garda

Garda Patrick Frawley – Stradbally garda

Garda William Murphy – Stradbally garda

Garda John Sullivan – Stradbally garda

Garda Commissioner General Eoin O'Duffy – head of An Garda Síochána

Deputy Commissioner Éamonn Coogan – deputy head of An Garda Síochána

Garda Chief Superintendent Harry O'Mara – in charge of Waterford garda division

Garda Superintendent James Hunt – investigating officer

Garda Superintendent Bernard Keenan – in charge of the Tramore garda district, including Stradbally

Garda Inspector Patrick McNamara – investigating officer

Garda Detective James Driscoll – investigating officer

Garda Detective Joseph Gantley – investigating officer

Garda Detective Thomas O'Rourke – one of the investigating gardaí

Patrick Whelan – publican

Bridget Whelan – wife of Patrick Whelan

James Whelan – son of Patrick and Bridget Whelan

Cissie Whelan – daughter of Patrick and Bridget Whelan

Nora Whelan – daughter of Patrick and Bridget Whelan

Thomas Cashin – school principal

Thomas (Tommy) Corbett – labourer living in James Fitzgerald's house

James (Jim) Fitzgerald – labourer living near Stradbally, known locally
    as Jim Greaney

Ned Morrissey – labourer and gravedigger

Jim Murphy – local man; was in Stradbally square on Christmas night

Larry O'Brien – local man; was in Stradbally square on Christmas night

John Power – local youth; was in Stradbally square on Christmas night

Paddy Power – local man; was in Stradbally square on Christmas night

Chapter 1

It was the worst winter Waterford had seen in many years, and the slightly built postman was bent almost double as he eased his mailbag onto his back and pointed his bicycle in the direction of Kilmacthomas.

'Desperate evening for it!'

As it was carried by the wind, Larry couldn't tell from which direction the voice had come. But its owner was, no doubt, headed in the direction of warmth, company and freshly poured beer. It was Christmas Eve 1929 and most of the inhabitants of the small village of Stradbally were making an early start to their Yuletide celebrations. Larry himself had the glow of several whiskeys inside him – Christmas was a busy time for the popular postman and many of his customers had sent him on his way with a glass of whiskey to shorten the road.

'Merry Christmas to you Larry!'

The bicycle wobbled precariously as Larry raised his hand to acknowledge another greeting. He had been travelling these roads for over fourteen years and, with his bow-legged gait and disabled arm, injured during his service in the Great War, was a familiar figure in the villages of Stradbally and Kilmacthomas.

For a moment, he thought of following the voice back towards the warmth and the companionship. But the night was growing colder and the following day, Christmas Day, would be for him the busiest of the working year. Pulling his coat closer around his shoulders he set his face towards the gale and began to cycle the eight miles home.

An hour later, having reported back to Kilmacthomas post office, Larry finally reached the warmth and safety of his own home at Millbrook terrace. His daughter Alice looked up from the hearth where she was wrapping the remaining Christmas presents and sighed when she saw how cold her father looked. But the postman batted away her concerns.

'Is Jack home?'

'He's inside in the bedroom this past hour.'

'And Mam?'

'She'll be down in a moment.'

The hall door opened and, needle in hand, Mary entered the kitchen. Her head was bowed and Larry, assuming it was the thought of their absent daughter Bridie that was upsetting her, smiled as she came towards him.

'She'll be fine. Many a girl from this parish will be eating their Christmas dinner in England this year.'

'It's not Bridie that's upsetting me.'

'What is it then? Ah, Mary … you're not going on with that oul rubbish again?'

'I'm not going to lie to you, Larry Griffin!'

She put her needlework down on the table, and stared defiantly at her husband of over twenty years.

'I've had that dream again. Six nights now, the same thing every time. You, covered in blood … in danger …'

Mary burst into tears as her husband and daughter looked on helplessly. Mary Griffin was a down-to-earth country woman, not given to flights of fancy or indeed overt shows of emotion. But the recurring dream she had been having about her husband had been disturbing her sleep for days, and left her shaken.

'Come on over here and get warm.'

Larry stretched out his hand and beckoned to her. After a moment, she smiled and went towards the fire. The wild weather had been left outside for the evening; it was Christmas Eve, time to relax and enjoy the family she had around her. Taking the cup of tea her daughter offered her, she pushed all thoughts of the nightmare to the back of her mind. But Mary Griffin did not know that this was the last Christmas she would spend with her husband, nor that the feelings of dread she had been experiencing would soon move from dreams to reality, and that she and her family would be the victims of the most shocking conspiracy and cover-up the young Irish state had yet known.

Chapter 2

—————◆—————

'You're too good Larry, you shouldn't have bothered.'

'Ah sure they're only little things for the young ones.'

It was 8.30 a.m. on Christmas morning and, having come back from mass, Larry had dropped in to his next-door neighbours, the McGraths, with presents for their two infant daughters, Delia and Cáit. Like Larry, their father Johnny McGrath was also a postman operating out of Kilmacthomas post office.

'You'll have a drop Larry.'

'Ah God no, it's too early for that, and sure you know yourself, they'll all be wanting me to have a sup today.'

After the visit to the McGraths Larry returned to his own house, where Jack and Alice were in high spirits, already looking forward to the Christmas-night dance in Bunmahon.

'What time are ye leaving for the dance tonight?' Larry asked them.

'About nine.'

'Wait till I get back from my rounds. I'll be back as soon as I can and I'll have a few half crowns for ye.'

Larry knew that there would be a fair few extra coins jangling in his pockets by the end of the day, for it was the tradition to give the postman money and to offer him the hospitality of the house as he went about his Christmas-day deliveries.

By midday Larry was cycling once more in blustery weather to Stradbally, merrily exchanging season's blessings with everyone he met on his way. The forty-nine-year-old postman's hair was grey, almost white, his face thin and his complexion reddish. He had a moustache and was missing several of his upper front teeth as well as a small part of his left ear.

Larry Griffin was born at Barrack Street, Waterford, the youngest member of a family of four boys and two girls. His father, who died when Larry was only five years old, was a Limerick man, and his mother a native of the parish of Ballyduff, County Waterford. Larry's wife Mary, to whom he had been married for twenty-two years, came from the area of Brownstown Head in East Waterford. The couple had three grown-up children – Jack, Bridie and Alice – as well as a son who had died at the age of eight and was buried in Knockboy cemetery, Waterford, and a daughter, Chrissie, who had died six years previously.

Larry was known as a man of strong religious faith who was a dedicated member of the Kilmacthomas Confraternity of the Sacred Heart and a regular communicant. He was a well-liked personality in the locality, in spite of his former service in the British army. He had enrolled with the Royal Artillery

Regiment in Belfast in 1899, and had served in India from 1901 to 1907. He later served in France during the Great War but after a shell splinter had permanently damaged his arm, he was discharged from the army. Considering the high death rate of troops on the Western Front, this injury may well have saved his life. The British post office in Ireland in pre-independence years had provided good steady jobs for many demobilised soldiers like Larry. While he now worked for the post office of the independent Irish state, many of the letters and parcels in his mailbag still bore British postage stamps with 'Rialtas Sealadach na hÉireann' crudely overprinted in black ink.

Larry entered the square at Stradbally by coming down the Chapel Road along a terrace of ruined houses, and he passed by Whelan's corner, named after the popular public house which stood where the Chapel Road met the square. Stradbally was, and still is, a typical Irish rural village – in fact the name Stradbally itself comes from the Irish *An tSráidbhaile*, meaning simply 'the village'. It lies about a half-mile from the coast between Dungarvan and Waterford city. At the end of the 1920s the normal population of the village was about 270 persons, with about another 400 living in the surrounding countryside, but this would have been swollen by adult sons and daughters visiting home for Christmas. The heart of Stradbally was a dirty, shabby square, with a water pump, a few trees and some crumbling stone walls in the centre of it.

Sometime during that afternoon Larry called to Whelan's

front door with letters for the two teenage Whelan girls – seventeen-year-old Nora and her nineteen-year-old sister Bridget, known to all as Cissie to distinguish her from her mother, also called Bridget. Their father, Patrick Whelan, a stout man of sixty years, was one of Stradbally's most prominent inhabitants, a publican as well as a farmer. No one else in the village could boast of having thirteen rooms in the main house as well as eleven outbuildings, including a barn, a dairy, a stable and a coach house. Patrick Whelan must have been a worried man that Christmas of 1929, however, for things had not been going well for his business. The hotel and pub trade had suffered since the War of Independence and the Civil War, and there had been a fall-off in the number of English visitors coming for the fishing. The introduction of more restrictive licensing laws by the then Minister for Justice Kevin O'Higgins in 1927 had not helped matters – the new legislation included a ban on the selling of alcohol on Christmas Day and Good Friday. Patrick Whelan was now in arrears with the rent due to his landlords, for he did not own his property outright. To make matters even worse he had been successfully sued by one of his suppliers, Thomas Murphy and Company of Clonmel, for non-payment for goods supplied, a humiliating blow for a man who had been a prosperous local businessman some years earlier.

While a photograph of Whelan's pub from 1910 shows an immaculately maintained shop front and pristine whitewashed walls, by 1929 the paint was fading and peeling away and the

23

building had a neglected run-down look about it. Around the time the earlier photograph was taken the Whelans had three employees living with them – two general labourers as well as a fifteen-year-old 'domestic nurse' or childminder. However, by 1929 they had no live-in employees, and three of the children were working on the farm and in the pub – the two girls Cissie and Nora, as well as twenty-year-old James. An older daughter, Mary, was working as a nurse in England and there was a younger son, Philip, who was just twelve years of age. As he contemplated the decade that was coming to an end, Patrick Whelan must have hoped that there would be better times ahead.

On the western side of the square, Larry called in to the home of another of Stradbally's most prominent citizens, forty-year-old Thomas Cashin, who was principal of the national school in Ballylaneen, about five miles away. As a school principal, with his third-level education, his salary of £260 a year and the only motor car in the village, Cashin enjoyed major status in the local community. His wife Kathleen also taught in the school, although she was not a qualified teacher, a common enough arrangement at the time. The couple had seven children. There was another side to Thomas Cashin, however. He had fought with the IRA during the War of Independence, had taken the anti-Treaty side during the Civil War and it was rumoured that he still had connections with the IRA, which was active in this part of Waterford. Thomas Cashin was a close friend of Patrick Whelan and a regular customer in his public house.

Larry Griffin may not have received as warm a welcome at the Cashin household as he did at his other stops that day, for there was bad blood between the postman and the school principal according to local folklore. The school principal, so the story goes, expected to have his mail delivered to him early in the morning before he left for work, but Larry, in the words of one local source, 'was one of those fellas who could meander along the road and have a chat and he was never here at 9 o'clock'. Cashin is supposed to have gone so far as to complain about Larry to the post office. The fact that Griffin was a former British soldier may have been another factor weighing against him in the mind of the republican veteran.

On his way back around the eastern side of the square Larry passed by the ruins of the old Royal Irish Constabulary (RIC) barracks, which had been burned down about ten years earlier during the War of Independence. Further up on this side of the square he delivered mail to the police force that had replaced the RIC at Stradbally barracks, which had a contingent of five gardaí, all of them in their twenties or early thirties. The youth of the Stradbally gardaí was typical of a force that had been hastily built up from scratch by the newly independent Irish state only a few years previously. Like most of their fellow gardaí, the Stradbally party were all veterans of the War of Independence, and had all supported the Free State when the IRA had split over the Anglo-Irish Treaty. They had been recruited primarily for their loyalty to the new state, but good guerrilla fighters did not necessarily make for competent police officers, despite the exhortations of their charismatic leader, Garda Commissioner General Eoin O'Duffy.

According to twenty-six-year-old Garda William Murphy, when Larry Griffin called in to the barracks on Christmas Day he had a few drinks taken but was not drunk:

> He asked me if there was any whiskey inside. I told him there was not a drop … From his demeanour towards me that afternoon and the fact that he had to visit other houses I would say that he would get drink at every house he would call to.

Next door to the garda barracks, Larry may have called in to the McGrath household and found several local men playing cards in what was known as 'the hall'. This was actually a front room in the house of Mike McGrath, which operated as a sort of low-cost card-playing club. Every Saturday night the McGraths would collect a weekly fee of sixpence from all the men who came there to play cards, and the hall was certainly open for business that Christmas Day. The McGraths also ran a shop in an extension at the side of the house.

Reflecting how well in Larry was with the locals, the Qeally family invited him to join them for Christmas dinner and a bottle of stout at about 2 p.m., but he was gone on his deliveries again by about 2.30 p.m. Around 3 p.m. he delivered a parcel to the Flynn family who lived in the square. The parcel was from one of the Flynn daughters who was in England and there was a charge of 5s 6d to be paid on it. Bridie Flynn, another daughter of the house, handed Larry two half-crowns and promised to give him the balance later. Around 3.20 p.m. he delivered mail to the Cunninghams in High Street. One of the daughters of the house, Kathleen, said that Larry was 'a bit jolly'. Larry was invited in for dinner again at about 5 p.m. by Bridget Brown when he called on her with some letters. He left Brown's at about 5.15 p.m. and shortly afterwards called on farmer John J. Cunningham who said that it 'was my intention to give Larry some intoxicating liquor, but on seeing Larry I considered he was intoxicated and I gave him no drink'. When he had finished his deliveries it was reported that Larry went, as was usual for him, to Stradbally post office, and stayed there until it was time to go home. At about 6.30 p.m. he left the post office. His wife Mary expected him home about nine o'clock.

By now the stormy weather of the previous night had died down, and for about three hours from 7 p.m. a fall of snow descended on the countryside. Nine o'clock came and went and still there was no sign of Larry at home in Kilmacthomas. As Mary looked anxiously out the window, the clouds drifted away, the night became exceptionally clear and the stars shone in all their mid-winter glory. Knowing that Larry would have had quite a few drinks on his rounds, Mary hoped that his non-appearance meant that he had decided to sleep it out in one of his many friends' houses, rather than attempt the eight miles home through the dark and snow. Mr Brown, the Kilmacthomas postmaster, had also been waiting for Larry to report back after his deliveries, and when there was no sign of him Brown called on Mrs Griffin sometime after midnight to enquire whether Larry had come straight home. When Mrs Griffin anxiously informed him that her husband had not arrived home, he said: 'Don't worry, there is no danger of him. He will be all right.' But, though she waited up all night, her husband, Larry Griffin the postman, did not come home that night, or ever again.

Chapter 3

David Connors was out for an early stroll on the road between Stradbally and Kilmacthomas at about 7.20 a.m. on St Stephen's morning. This particular stretch of the road was straight for about a mile, bordered by ditches and totally exposed apart from a few nearby trees, their branches bare and leafless at this time of year.

As he moved closer to the Five Crossroads and Stradbally village, his breath visible in the frosty air, there wasn't another soul to be seen. But something in the distance caught his eye – a black object lying in the middle of the road. Curious to know the nature of the mysterious object, Connors quickened his pace. As he neared it, the mysterious object took on the form of a black bicycle. When he finally stood over it, at a spot about two miles from Stradbally village, Connors recognised it as a postman's bicycle, due to the distinctive carrier in front of the handlebars where the postbag was normally transported. Connors also knew, as did everyone in the district, that Larry Griffin was the postman who travelled this route. But he was puzzled, as there was no sign of Larry. The bicycle seemed to have been put down carefully about three feet from the right-hand side of the road, and it was facing towards Kilmacthomas.

The gardaí were informed of the discovery, but it was believed at first that the postman must have stayed the night in some house in the locality, sleeping off the effects of drink. However, as the morning wore on and Griffin did not surface, it began to be suspected, by both the gardaí and the missing man's friends, that he had come to harm. Two postmen from Kilmacthomas, Frank Cashin and Larry's next-door neighbour Johnny McGrath, came to Stradbally in a pony and trap looking for Larry. They were accompanied by another Kilmacthomas man, Tony Cullinane. The local gardaí in Stradbally also started searching for Larry and the school principal, Thomas Cashin, offered to drive two of them, Edward Dullea and William Murphy, around the storm-lashed countryside as they carried out their enquiries. Superintendent Bernard Keenan from Tramore organised a search party of gardaí from Stradbally, Kilmacthomas and Leamybrien stations, and they were joined by over a hundred civilian volunteers, including the missing postman's son, Jack. They searched the whole countryside between Kilmacthomas and Stradbally and they paid particular attention to the marsh lands known as the Glen Bog, which adjoined either side of the road near where Larry's bicycle was found.

The main theory at this early stage of the investigation was that Griffin had wandered off the road in a drunken state and fallen into one of the very deep holes in the bog. But one of the postmen from Kilmacthomas examined Larry's bicycle and noticed something odd: an empty mailbag, a waterproof cover, a pair of overalls and a cycling cape were all strapped on the carrier and folded neatly. It was very unusual for any postman to strap his cape on the carrier because it tended to crack when it was folded up. For this reason the cape would usually be slung loosely over the letter pouch. The Kilmacthomas postman also noticed that the back wheel of the bicycle was flat.

The searches continued over the following days despite the continuing strong winds, and falls of sleet and rain. Extra gardaí were brought in from other stations to assist and hundreds of civilians trudged through muddy and waterlogged farmland for miles around in the search for the postman. All pools in the Glen Bog were dragged, and every possible place into which Larry might have accidentally strayed along his way was thoroughly examined. The parish priest of Stradbally, Fr John Lannon, appealed to the farmers of the parish to search their lands, but not the slightest trace of Larry could be found.

The disappearance of the postman was reported to Chief Superintendent Harry O'Mara of Waterford on 27 December and he visited Stradbally that evening. O'Mara, thirty-three years of age and married with four children, was one of many young men who had risen rapidly to positions of prominence in the new state due to his role in the struggle for independence. A native of County Clare, he had initially studied for the priesthood in Maynooth, deciding after three years that he didn't have a vocation. In 1918 he entered University College Dublin (UCD) to study medicine, but this too had to be abandoned as he became increasingly involved in both the political and the military wings of the revolutionary movement. He rose to the rank of adjutant of the East Clare IRA Brigade and was also a member of Clare County Council. O'Mara joined the gardaí soon after the foundation of the force in February 1922 (initially called the Civic Guard), once the new state had been set up. Within one month he was promoted to the rank of superintendent, and later to that of chief superintendent.

When he reached Stradbally barracks, O'Mara questioned the local gardaí about Larry Griffin's movements on Christmas Day and asked them who had last seen the postman. He also wanted to know if any of them had seen Larry leave the village on Christmas Day. Not one of them said that he had seen the postman leave the village.

The sergeant, James Cullinane, told the chief superintendent that he and Garda Patrick Frawley had gone on patrol to the neighbouring village of Bunmahon that evening. Garda Ned Dullea told him that a local man, Larry O'Brien, was supposed to have met Larry Griffin between Stradbally and the Five Crossroads, on Christmas evening, about a mile from Stradbally on the Kilmacthomas Road. This seemed to indicate that Larry had left the village and started his journey homeward. O'Mara asked whether Larry Griffin was drunk or sober on the evening of Christmas Day and they told him that they understood Griffin was sober. Garda Dullea in particular seemed eager to point out that the postman was known to have been sober. Nobody with any knowledge of the case, especially the local gardaí, could have been in any doubt that it was crucial to establish what Larry Griffin's last movements were, and who had seen him last.

As the postman's family continued to suffer the torment of not knowing what had happened to him, on 29 December a number of men were brought to the garda station and closely questioned as to whether they had seen Larry on Christmas night between the village and the place where his bicycle was found. According to Chief Superintendent O'Mara's account:

A number of labourers had been playing cards up to a late hour in a house quite near to where the bicycle was found and we questioned those very hard but they satisfied us that they hadn't seen either himself or the bicycle.

Meanwhile gardaí were brought from other stations to help organise search parties, despite the almost continual storms and rains that prevailed at the end of December and at the beginning of January 1930. Every inch of the bog near where Griffin's bicycle was found was carefully probed with specially made poles, and the cliffs and seashore from Bunmahon to Dungarvan were searched. All the nearby garda stations were also making enquiries. It was established that a sister of Larry's lived in Belfast where he had enlisted in the British army many years before. The gardaí alerted the Royal Ulster Constabulary in Belfast to Larry Griffin's disappearance and asked them to make enquiries to find out if he was in the city. They also circulated the postman's description to police forces in western England and Wales in case his body might be washed ashore there.

Chief Superintendent O'Mara was baffled by the case as all the obvious possibilities seemed to rule themselves out. Did Larry commit suicide by drowning himself in a bog-hole? It was usual for those committing suicide by drowning to divest themselves of coat and cap, but there was no trace of these. And of course his body could not be found in the bog. Larry had never shown any indication of mental ill health and there was no history of such problems in his family. As far as could be ascertained he had no financial, family or health problems. It also seemed unlikely, therefore, that he had absconded of his own free will. Had the postman been attacked for the purposes of robbery? There was no sign of a struggle and it was well known that he would have no official money on his return journey. Had he been struck by a motor car? The bicycle was undamaged and there were no bloodstains or other marks on the road. Had he wandered in a drunken state and died in some other location? About six years previously, around Christmas time, he had been found in a drunken state going in the direction of Dungarvan and it was with some difficulty that he was persuaded he was not going to Kilmacthomas. But all the farmers for miles around the vicinity had searched their lands and the gardaí had carefully searched a radius of five or six miles.

O'Mara now began to suspect foul play was involved, but for some motive other than robbery. While a possible murder or abduction would be a serious matter at any time, the fact that Larry Griffin was a postman meant that this case would be given particular attention. The Garda Síochána and the other institutions of the state were still only a few years old and there were those who were willing and able to undermine the new order through the force of arms. In July 1927, as he made his way to Sunday mass in Booterstown in County Dublin, the Minister for Justice Kevin O'Higgins had been assassinated by an IRA faction. The IRA had also killed several gardaí in the preceding years and it was believed that they had killed a postman who had gone missing the previous year in County Clare and had never been found. 'Postmen, by virtue of their profession, saw and heard a lot,' writes Tadhg Ó Dúshláine. 'In the aftermath of the civil war they were often seen as arms of the Free State and often falsely accused by republicans of being informers.' An attack on a postman, therefore, was seen by the authorities as an attack on the state itself.

As the enquiries progressed O'Mara's suspicions intensified. It was ascertained that on his return journey to Kilmacthomas the postman used to call at the Convent of Mercy, Stradbally, where he would collect the mail from a bag attached to a fixture outside the convent gate. The mail was hung out for collection as normal on Christmas Day. It was usually called for between 7.10 p.m. and 7.20 p.m. However, it was not collected that evening and the bag and contents were taken back into the convent shortly after 10 p.m. the same night. Further out from Stradbally on the postman's homeward journey, just 200 yards before the place where the bicycle was found, was a cottage known as the 'Half-Way House', occupied by Mrs Walsh. Farmers from the district were accustomed to leaving letters at this house for collection, and Larry Griffin called every day on his outward and return journey. He did not call there on Christmas night, however, which suggested that he never got as far as the cottage. Furthermore, if Larry had left Stradbally at 6.30 p.m. and had abandoned his bicycle on the narrow country road two miles out from the village, it is likely that a passer-by would have spotted it at some stage before the next morning. However, a young man who passed along the road at about 4 a.m. coming from a dance in Bunmahon declared emphatically that there was no bicycle there at that time. O'Mara now began to consider the possibility that the bicycle had been deliberately placed on the road as a diversion.

O'Mara was in close touch with Fr O'Shea, one of three priests in the parish of Stradbally, all of whom would feature in some way in the case of the missing postman. The parish priest Fr Lannon and another priest, Fr Burke, were based in Stradbally village, while Fr O'Shea had only recently moved into a house in the neighbouring village of Ballylaneen – in fact he was the first ever resident priest in that village. A priest was a very important and influential person in a rural Irish community of the time, and it seems that Fr O'Shea was doing his best to use his position of trust among the people to gather information that might be of assistance in the investigation.

On 6 January Fr O'Shea sent for Chief Superintendent O'Mara and made a dramatic assertion about Larry Griffin's disappearance which was to alter the course of the enquiry entirely. The priest alleged to O'Mara 'that the gardaí in Stradbally were concealing what occurred and that I should question them closely but before doing so that I should question a young lad named Power who, he said, had seen Griffin on the night of his disappearance'. The young lad referred to was sixteen-year-old John Power.

The allegation by such a trusted source of some sort of cover-up on the part of local gardaí was taken very seriously by O'Mara and by Garda Commissioner General O'Duffy to whom he passed on the allegation. The unarmed and impartial approach of An Garda Síochána had been a vital element in gaining public trust and returning the country to peace and normality after the violence and lawlessness of the War of Independence and Civil War. With the threat of IRA violence lurking in the background, the fear of a breakdown of law and order was a powerful motivating factor in the Free State administration. The reputation and loyalty of the gardaí were seen as vital in avoiding this, and any hint of that reputation or loyalty being undermined was bound to be treated with the utmost seriousness.

The next morning, O'Mara went early to Stradbally garda station accompanied by a detective and a garda sergeant; he was met at the station by two senior officers, Superintendent O'Shea of Dungarvan and Superintendent Keenan of Tramore. Stradbally was part of the Tramore garda district. John Power was sent for and O'Mara personally questioned him in the presence of the other officers.

John Power told O'Mara that he had been on the street at the window of Whelan's public house from about 6 p.m. on Christmas Day. Three other local men, Jim Murphy, Larry O'Brien and Paddy Power, had also been at Whelan's corner, he said. John Power then made the astonishing revelation that he had seen the missing postman in the company of one of the local gardaí outside the post office in the centre of Stradbally at about 6.30 p.m. on Christmas Day: 'They [Dullea and Griffin] passed up and went on to the Chapel Road. They were talking. The bicycle was nearest to us, pushed by Guard Dullea, and Griffin was on the outside.' This was the same Garda Dullea who had been left in no doubt by Chief Superintendent O'Mara that it was vital to establish Larry Griffin's last movements and ascertain who had seen him last. Yet he had failed to reveal that he himself had been with the postman on the evening of his disappearance. Furthermore, according to Power, the postman was 'leaning his arm on Dullea's shoulder'. Power thought that Griffin 'was like a fellow who would be drunk'. He added that when the postman was going around the corner 'he was trying to discharge of his stomach'. Garda Dullea had told Chief Superintendent O'Mara that the postman was sober when he left the village, but, according to Power, not only was Griffin clearly drunk, but Dullea himself must have known this.

Power said that he had remained at Whelan's corner for an hour and that he did not see Dullea again: 'I would have seen him if he passed back. None of us looked after them up the Chapel Road.' So Dullea was now the last known person to have been in Larry Griffin's company as the drunken postman started up the Chapel Road, apparently on his way home.

The dramatic evidence about Garda Dullea and the missing postman led to a frenetic burst of activity in Stradbally garda station that day. The other men who had been at Whelan's corner with John Power – Jim Murphy, Larry O'Brien and Paddy Power – were brought in for questioning and they all backed up John Power's account.

Garda Dullea was hauled in for questioning. Like Chief Superintendent Harry O'Mara, twenty-nine-year-old Ned Dullea, a native of County Cork, had joined An Garda Síochána in the early days of the new force. However, unlike O'Mara, the tall, fair-haired young man had not displayed any particular ability or initiative and had not risen through the ranks. Dullea admitted to meeting Larry Griffin outside the post office at about 6.30 p.m. on Christmas Day. As to why he hadn't mentioned this before, all he could come up with was that he had 'thought it was of no importance'. Bearing in mind how clearly O'Mara had emphasised to Dullea and the other Stradbally guards the importance of establishing Griffin's last movements, this statement is simply unbelievable, especially coming from a member of An Garda Síochána.

Dullea still insisted that the postman had not been drunk and that he 'appeared to me to be quite normal in every way'. Contrary to the evidence of other witnesses who had seen them, Dullea claimed that it was the postman himself who was pushing the bicycle, implying that he was sober enough to do so. Dullea gave his interrogators an account of his conversation with Griffin:

> I asked Griffin was it now he was going home. He said yes. I asked him would he want a lamp for his bicycle. He said no, he was not supplied with lamps and he preferred to be without one. I walked about fifty yards up the Kilmacthomas Road with him – just to the first turn above the corner. I then came back to the village and he carried on towards Kilmacthomas. He was walking. We met nobody and I saw no one until I reached Whelan's corner and the same men were at Whelan's.

This account directly contradicts John Power's statement that Dullea could not have come back around the corner without Power seeing him. Nor did any of the other witnesses see Dullea come back after he had gone around the corner with Griffin. Dullea was clearly still not telling the full truth, and he seemed nervous to O'Mara.

Dullea claimed that having returned to the centre of the village he waited to meet a girl he was courting, nineteen-year-old Cissie Whelan of Whelan's public house. He said that Cissie came to meet him after five minutes, that they went for a walk towards Stradbally Cove, and returned at about 10 p.m. John Power, however, said that this could not have happened: 'If any of the Whelan girls were at the door that night I would have seen them. I would have seen a couple meeting at the corner, but I did not see any couple.' None of the other witnesses saw the courting couple either. As they continued to probe him and try to find out what he was hiding, his interrogators suggested to Dullea that he must have gone into Whelan's for illicit drinks on Christmas Day. Dullea denied this and said that he hadn't set foot in the public house at all that day. At this point in the interview, however, it seems the pressure of whatever secret he was keeping finally became too much for Dullea: he fainted and fell to the floor. The interview had to be abandoned.

Cissie Whelan backed up Garda Dullea's account in every respect when she was questioned. She also said that when she returned home at about 10 p.m., having been to the cove with

Dullea, there was no one else anywhere in the house apart from her own family. Indeed all the members of the Whelan family who were interviewed denied that there was anyone other than themselves in the house that day, and denied that any drink had been served. They said that Larry Griffin had not called in to them at all on Christmas Day, despite the fact that he had done so on every previous Christmas Day for the past fourteen years.

There was another aspect to John Power's statement which greatly troubled Chief Superintendent O'Mara. He said that a few days after Christmas Day he met Larry O'Brien and Paddy Power again at Whelan's corner. O'Brien told the other men that he had had an unwelcome visit from Garda Murphy of the Stradbally barracks: 'He told us Guard Murphy had been with him … and told him he'd be summoned and that he should get two witnesses to prove he saw Dullea with Larry Griffin.' Another of those present also heard O'Brien say this and added that O'Brien had asked them 'not to speak of it'.

Talk of being summoned and having to find witnesses to back up his statement would have been very frightening to a country labourer like O'Brien, with limited formal education, and Garda Murphy would have known this. The evidence seemed to suggest that Garda Murphy was trying to frighten the witness into staying silent about what he had seen. Furthermore, it seemed to indicate that Garda Murphy was also withholding information from the investigating officers.

The investigating gardaí confirmed that twenty-six-year-old Garda Murphy, a pro-treaty IRA veteran from County Limerick, had indeed visited Larry O'Brien. When they questioned O'Brien he admitted telling the other men that Garda Murphy had told him he would be summoned if he did not 'whist up' but he now said that this wasn't true. He had no explanation to offer, however, as to why he would have told such a lie. All he could come up with was: 'I do not know why I said that.' Garda Murphy described the allegation as 'baseless and malicious' and called O'Brien a fool and an idiot. There was no apparent reason for O'Brien to make up such an allegation and O'Mara was inclined to believe that O'Brien had been telling the truth when he spoke to the other men, and that Garda Murphy had in fact tried to intimidate the witness.

Garda Murphy gave an account of his movements on Christmas Day which involved going on patrol and returning to the barracks about 9 p.m.; this ruled out being in Whelan's public house at any time. He backed up Garda Dullea's claim that Dullea returned to the barracks at about 10.30 p.m., that he was sober and that he did not go out again after that.

Garda Murphy, however, contradicted Dullea on another point. Dullea and Murphy had dinner together in the barracks on Christmas Day around 2 p.m. Dullea admitted that there was a bottle of whiskey and a bottle of wine in the barracks and owned up to drinking some of the wine himself. However, Murphy said that 'Guard Dullea took no drink that day' and claimed that he 'never saw any drink in the barracks'. This has been described as the 'most ridiculous statement I have seen for a long time' by a former senior garda detective who has reviewed the witness evidence in the case. It was common for alcohol to be present and consumed in garda stations on Christmas Day, despite it being a breach of regulations. However, the more important point is that this was the first conflict of evidence to be discovered between the statements of Stradbally gardaí about Christmas Day, and it was not to be the last.

Even the evidence of the sergeant in charge of Stradbally barracks now began to unravel. Sergeant Cullinane had given Chief Superintendent O'Mara a statement in which he had said that he had raided Whelan's pub once on Christmas night, about 6 p.m. Other witnesses, however, testified that they had seen him enter Whelan's pub a second time, shortly afterwards. Even when faced with this contradictory evidence Cullinane insisted at first that he had only been in Whelan's once. He eventually conceded that he had in fact raided Whelan's a second time, at about 6.35 p.m. The reason for his second raid was to see if he could catch Gardaí Dullea, Frawley and Murphy drinking on the premises. He said that Gardaí Dullea and Murphy in particular were a source of constant trouble to him with regard to frequenting Whelan's public house, and this was borne out by other witnesses who said that Dullea and Murphy spent 'every spare minute they had' in Whelan's. Cullinane said he had lied about his second raid because he had not wanted to admit the extent of the disciplinary problems in Stradbally to his superior officers.

Such disciplinary problems were not infrequent in the early years of An Garda Síochána. As Gregory Allen points out in his history of the force, it was difficult for General O'Duffy and his senior officers to establish discipline 'among thousands of young, inexperienced recruits scattered in small units under youthful sergeants, depending on their bicycles as the only means of transport for maintaining contact with colleagues in neighbouring stations'. The recruits, Allen points out, had regular money in their pockets, many of them for the first time in their lives: 'Beset by boredom, and suffering real privation in appalling living conditions, it was not surprising that some of the young guards resorted to the public houses that dotted the countryside in unconscionable numbers at that period.'[1] O'Duffy explicitly recognised the problem when he issued a general order on 'Intemperance in the Civic Guard' in December 1922, in which he wrote that a certain proportion 'of the guard is developing or has developed a certain notoriety for drinking, and for frequenting the company of tipplers'. O'Duffy took a strong stance against such behaviour among his recruits, and Sergeant Cullinane would have been well aware that standards in Stradbally had fallen far short of what was expected.

As well as his evidence about Dullea, Murphy and Frawley, Cullinane also said that on both visits to Whelan's on the evening of Christmas Day, he found only the members of the Whelan

---

1   Gregory Allen (1999), p. 84

family on the premises. Mrs Whelan, however, continued to insist that Sergeant Cullinane had only raided the pub once. It seemed obvious to Chief Superintendent O'Mara that Mrs Whelan had been coached on what she was to say in her statement, and it strengthened his belief that there was a cover-up going on. But what exactly was being covered up by the Stradbally gardaí? In a report to General O'Duffy, O'Mara outlined two possible scenarios:

(a) When the Postman disappeared they were anxious to conceal the fact that he was drunk and that they were the last to see him depart in case that disciplinary action might be taken against them for knowingly allowing him to proceed in such a condition, or

(b) That he died from the effects of drink while in Garda Dullea's presence.

The Stradbally gardaí were now all suspects in the disappearance of Larry Griffin and, with General O'Duffy himself paying attention to the case, the pressure on them was mounting. And young John Power was about to cause them even more trouble.

Chapter 4

As January progressed, dark storm clouds continued to gather over Stradbally. A fall of snow on Saturday 11 January gave way to violent gales and rains over the following two days. It seemed as if there had been little respite from the storms since November, and the newspapers carried many reports of floods and damage to property in County Waterford.

As more witnesses in the Larry Griffin case gave statements, and as some of those who had previously been questioned added more details to their evidence, a clear picture emerged of what had happened in the centre of Stradbally between 6 p.m. and 7 p.m. on Christmas Day, although the rest of the night continued to be shrouded in mystery.

Shortly after 6 p.m. a clearly drunk Larry Griffin, accompanied by Garda Dullea, had called into the flat of Garda Patrick Frawley above the post office and next door to Whelan's pub in Stradbally square. Thirty-three-year-old Garda Frawley, a native of County Clare, was a married man and father of two children. He lived with his wife Brigid and their children.

Garda Frawley was wearing his garda uniform as he was

on duty that day, while Garda Dullea was in civilian clothes. Mrs Brigid Frawley gave the men some drink. After a while the three men left the house and stood on the street outside. Sergeant Cullinane could see the three men from where he was standing at Byrne's corner but he did not recognise Garda Dullea in the dark and out of uniform.

Frawley and Dullea discussed what to do about Larry Griffin as it was clear he was too drunk to make his way home eight miles to Kilmacthomas. Frawley said he would go to Whelan's to see 'if the coast was clear' and to ask them if they would put Larry up for the night. He then walked up the street, past John Power and the other men standing at Whelan's corner, and entered Whelan's by the back door. But the coast was not clear: Sergeant Cullinane spotted Frawley entering Whelan's and followed him in, suspecting that he and Dullea, and perhaps Garda Murphy too, were drinking in the pub. Realising that the sergeant had followed him, Frawley quickly exited the pub and returned to Dullea and Griffin, and told Dullea that the sergeant was about. Frawley then went back to his own flat. The sergeant came out of Whelan's, not having found the guards drinking there, and returned to where he had previously been standing at Byrne's corner. Then Garda Dullea and Griffin started walking from Frawley's house towards Whelan's corner. Griffin was leaning on Dullea's shoulder and trying to vomit, and Dullea was pushing the bicycle. Most importantly, it now emerged that, after they had gone around the corner, Dullea and Griffin went in through Whelan's back gate and were not seen to emerge again. In other words, barring the unlikely possibility that they had spent several hours in Whelan's backyard on a cold winter night, Garda Dullea and Larry Griffin had gone into Whelan's public house through the back door.

Just like Garda Dullea, Garda Frawley had omitted to tell Chief Superintendent Harry O'Mara any of this vital information when the latter had first come to the village. Frawley had also left it out of his formal statements, which made him guilty of assisting Dullea in a cover-up and of obstructing the investigation into Larry Griffin's disappearance.

As the investigating officers started to put more pressure on the local Stradbally gardaí, further conflicts began to emerge in their evidence. As mentioned in the previous chapter, one of these conflicts of evidence revolved around the issue of alcohol being consumed in the barracks on Christmas Day. Both Sergeant Cullinane and Garda Sullivan said that on Christmas Eve a bottle of whiskey and a bottle of wine were received at the station from a publican in Bunmahon, Miss Curran. They said that Sullivan took delivery of the parcel containing the whiskey and wine and that he then gave it to Garda Murphy. But Murphy denied this:

> It is a lie to say that I took charge of the whiskey and wine which came from Miss Curran of Bunmahon by bus. It would be a lie if Guard Sullivan said that he took it from the bus and handed

it to me ... I have no idea of what happened to the bottle of
wine.

Garda Dullea said that he and Garda Murphy had some of the
wine and whiskey on Christmas Day when they were taking
their dinner in the barracks around 2 p.m., but Garda Murphy
also denied this. While the consumption of a few drinks in the
barracks on Christmas Day as described in most of the statements
would have been a breach of regulations, it was known to be a
widespread practice. It might have resulted in disciplinary action
but it would not have gone as far as dismissal from the force or
permanent damage to careers. In a situation where a man was
missing, presumed dead, and foul play was suspected, one would
imagine that innocent men would tell the truth about such
relatively minor infringements. Yet it was clear that lies were
being told, leading the investigating officers to believe that there
was more to the question of drink in the barracks than they were
being led to believe.

The cosy relationship these statements suggest between the
Stradbally gardaí and local publicans is also of interest. The sergeant and Garda Frawley went on patrol to Bunmahon on Christmas night but they didn't raid the pub of Miss Curran, who had
sent them the gift of whiskey and wine. The investigating officers
must have known that a similarly close relationship was likely to
have existed with the local publicans in Stradbally itself, including
Whelan's, and that this could be an important factor in the case.

It also became clear that lies were being told by some of the Stradbally gardaí about the station diary. All official comings and goings in the station had to be recorded contemporaneously in the diary. These would include officers going on and returning from patrol, officers going on and coming off duty, roll calls and other official business. At first glance it appeared that the entries in the diary confirmed the accounts of their movements given by the various gardaí on the day. For instance, Garda Dullea said that he came back from leave on Christmas Day at 10.30 p.m., that he called the roll in the station and that they all went to bed after that. Gardaí Murphy and Sullivan both said they were present when Dullea returned and called the roll. When the investigators examined the station diary, it seemed to confirm this version of events.

However, when they examined the records in the diary for the next morning, St Stephen's Day, they noticed that one entry had been erased and that a new entry had been written in its place. Sergeant Cullinane at first tried to explain this away as a simple mix-up which occurred on the morning of St Stephen's Day between himself and the barrack orderly Garda Sullivan. However, under further intense questioning Sergeant Cullinane gave a totally different explanation for the altered entry:

Next morning St Stephen's day ... I saw that there was no Roll Call recorded at 11 p.m. on 25 December 1929. Just at this time (at the time when I noticed these omissions) Guard O'Sullivan [*sic*] remarked to me 'that Dullea must have forgot to call the Roll last night'.

The sergeant said that an hour later when he was about to make another entry in the diary, he noticed that a record of the 11 p.m. roll call for Christmas Day had suddenly appeared:

I noticed that it was in Guard Dullea's handwriting and signed by him … I asked Dullea why he made the entry of Roll Call on 25 December 1929 on page 69. He just looked at it then and said I forgot to put it in last night and I have put it in the wrong place so I don't know what we will do with it. That's all he said. I said I don't know either. I just told him to put it on page 68 and he did so. I rubbed out the Roll Call on page 69.

Garda Dullea backed up this new version of events. Sergeant Cullinane said that his reason for lying was that he knew he was guilty of breaches of the regulations for not taking disciplinary action against the guards concerned over the omissions in the diary. He said he had 'let them off' because it was Christmas night and that he was 'not overzealous in reporting Breaches of the Regulations other than … drinking and visiting Whelan's Public House'.

The investigators, however, still believed that Sergeant Cullinane was not telling the full truth. They were convinced that he was in fact covering up more serious irregularities which had occurred in the station on Christmas night, and that this was somehow connected with the disappearance of the postman. Did Dullea really return to the barracks at 10.30 p.m. on Christmas night? And if he did, did he really stay in the barracks and not go out again? Was Garda Murphy in the barracks that night? These suspicions were further heightened when Garda Sullivan continued to insist that all entries had been properly recorded in the diary on Christmas night:

> I would be surprised to hear that the sergeant has stated that neither the 11.00 p.m. Roll Call or the return of the sergeant and Guard Frawley which now appear on page 68 of the Diary were not there at 9 a.m. on the 26th and if he stated any such thing it is a lie and a most extraordinary lie too. If Guard Dullea bore out the sergeant regarding what he said about those entries it would be a lie and a most extraordinary one. If Guard Dullea said that those entries had not been made at 9 o'clock on the morning of 26.12.29 it would be a lie. It would be a lie if he said they were not in at 8 a.m. on that morning. It would be a lie if any one said that the Roll was not called at all.

Not only were the Stradbally gardaí changing their stories as they went along, they were contradicting each other's evidence and now calling each other liars as well. And their credibility crumbled further when it was proven that other patrols they claimed to have carried out on Christmas Day could not have happened as they described.

Garda Murphy claimed to have been on patrol from 5 p.m. until 8.30 p.m. When questioned regarding who he had seen while on patrol he claimed to have spotted a motor car driven by John Rowe of Ballylynch, Kilmacthomas, and to have met a man called John Fitzsimmons. Even though Rowe and Fitzsimmons contradicted this, Murphy continued to insist that it was the truth. O'Mara wrote that he 'shows self confidence and endeavours to display that he is sure and exact about everything but he is essentially evasive'. Just as Garda Dullea was courting Cissie Whelan, Garda Murphy was courting her seventeen-year-old sister Nora. O'Mara believed it was reasonable to assume that Murphy had spent the time between 5 p.m. and 8.30 p.m. on Christmas Day in the company of Nora Whelan, and not on patrol as he was supposed to have been. Furthermore, while Garda Murphy claimed that he spent the rest of Christmas night after 8 p.m. in the barracks, the barrack orderly John Sullivan said that Murphy returned to the barracks at 10.30 p.m. with Garda Dullea. All this led O'Mara to believe 'that if the gardaí had, for any motive, anything to do with the disposal of the body, that Guard Murphy was principally responsible and suggested the line of action'.

Garda Frawley was supposed to have left on patrol at 2 p.m. on Christmas Day and to have taken a predetermined route via several local townlands. Again, he was supposed to have seen a particular motor car, but when this was proven not to be the case he admitted that he had 'concocted that entry of the patrol in the patrol book'. He now claimed to have stayed in the vicinity of Stradbally village and the nearby cove: 'The reason I did not record my visit to the Cove was that there was nothing of importance and it is not included on the list of places on patrol "B" on which I was supposed to be.' However, he claimed not to have met anyone on this alternative patrol, and so nobody could confirm his new account.

Garda Frawley, as already noted, was a married man who lived with his wife in a flat over the post office. Sergeant Culli- nane was unmarried and lived in the barracks. Garda Frawley's sister-in-law, Hannah Griffin, from Ballinaspittle in County Cork, was staying with Frawley and his wife for a few weeks, and Sergeant Cullinane had begun courting her. As already mentioned, Sergeant Cullinane and Garda Frawley had gone on patrol to Bunmahon on Christmas night. According to them, they returned to the barracks at midnight and Garda Frawley went home while Sergeant Cullinane went straight to bed. Garda Peter Twamley, however, one of the officers brought in from Waterford to take over the investigation, had previ- ously served in Stradbally and had a good rapport with the people there. Twamley reported a conversation he had with a local man, John Flynn, which contradicted Cullinane and Frawley's story. John Flynn told Garda Twamley that 'Guard Frawley's sister-in-law used to visit his [Flynn's] house every evening and since the postman got lost she asked them not to give any information to the guards about him [Frawley].' She also said that when the sergeant and Frawley returned from Bunmahon, they came into Frawley's house and the sergeant did not go home until 6.00 a.m. the next morning. Garda Frawley continued to insist that he and Sergeant Cullinane parted company at the end of the Bunmahon patrol and that he did not see the sergeant again that night:

> It would be a lie to say that the sergeant went into my house that night after coming back from Bunmahon. My sister-in-law was in the house that night and she was in bed when I came in. My wife was preparing to go to bed and I went to bed immediately. Even if my sister-in-law or my wife said that the sergeant was in my house that night it would be a lie. The sergeant was not in my house as far as I know on Christmas day.

However, the Frawleys and Hannah Griffin were later forced to admit that Sergeant Cullinane had in fact come back to the house that night, although they continued to try to downplay the session, claiming that the sergeant had left at 11.30 p.m. having had only one bottle of stout and that they were all in their beds by midnight.

Chief Superintendent O'Mara had heard enough lies. He was now convinced that the Stradbally gardaí were involved in the disappearance of Larry Griffin and that it was time to take action against them. He reported to General O'Duffy that Gardaí Dullea and Murphy 'are influencing the people to make false statements or abstain from making the statements and are visiting those from whom statements have been taken to ascertain what they have said'. He told General O'Duffy that the entire Stradbally party would never prove useful as policemen and that their presence in Stradbally was only hampering the investigation. The garda commissioner agreed and the fate of the Stradbally garda contingent was sealed. In mid-January, with very little notice, they were all transferred to various garda stations in other parts of Ireland and were replaced by two detectives and a large contingent of gardaí from Waterford city. Garda Dullea was posted to the garda depot in the Phoenix Park in Dublin, Garda Murphy was sent to County Mayo, Garda Sullivan to County Limerick, Garda Frawley to County Cavan and Sergeant Cullinane to County Kerry. However, O'Mara was convinced that the Stradbally guards and the Whelans would try to communicate with each other about the case, and he felt that useful information could be obtained by intercepting their mail. General O'Duffy agreed and a warrant was sought from, and granted by, the Minister for Justice to allow this interception.

Chapter 5

————◆————

Whether as rumour, fact or surmise, everybody in Stradbally knew by now that something had happened to Larry Griffin in Whelan's pub on Christmas night. It was only a matter of time before some of these stories started coming back to the investigating officers. While some of the details of the stories varied, they all agreed that Larry Griffin was drinking in Whelan's pub late on Christmas night, that he was very drunk, and that there were two guards in the pub at the time. One local woman, Mrs McGrath, when chatting with two of the garda replacements posted to the village, said that she too had heard that the postman had been in Whelan's on Christmas night and she then made the following cryptic remark: 'It is no crime for a man to die if they only treated him as they should.' Try as they might, the two guards were unable to get any more information out of her.

However, a very significant piece of evidence came in statements from the three men from Kilmacthomas who had come to Stradbally looking for Larry Griffin on St Stephen's Day. These were the two postmen, Frank Cashin and Johnny McGrath, and the third man, Tony Cullinane. When they came to Whelan's pub, Patrick Whelan was standing at the door and they told him they were looking for Larry. According to Frank Cashin, Whelan confirmed that Larry had been in the pub the night before. The publican said: 'I wanted him [Larry Griffin] to stay for the night and he would not stay by any means.' Tony Cullinane's statement backed this up: 'During the conversation he [Mr Whelan] said that when Larry Griffin was going out home he tried to stop him and make him remain for the night.' Having spoken to Whelan, Frank Cashin had gone into the pub for a drink:

> One of the girls, I think it was Cissie, served me. I asked her some questions concerning Larry Griffin and she said, 'I went up the road as far as the convent with him and he was very heavy or very happy.' I don't know whether she said heavy or happy but I understood her to mean that Griffin was intoxicated. She spoke in a rather low voice which gave me the impression that she did not want the public to know.

The Whelans' comments to the Kilmacthomas men on St Stephen's Day were at odds with their later denials to the gardaí that drink had been served in breach of the licensing laws or that Larry Griffin had been on the premises on Christmas Day, and in O'Mara's view this pointed to 'a guilty knowledge'. It is surprising, however, that their earlier comments were made rather publicly. O'Mara felt that this change in attitude might be explained 'by a desire to save the guards', although one would have thought that the prospect of being prosecuted for breaching the licensing laws would have been motive enough.

Another possible indication of a guilty knowledge on the part of the Whelan family also occurred around this time. Larry Griffin's daughter Bridie and his sister-in-law Anastasia had both come home from England when they had heard about his disappearance. One day they walked to Stradbally and called into Whelan's. As they had never met the Whelans before, Anastasia introduced herself and turning to Bridie said: 'This is Larry's daughter.' Cissie Whelan started crying and left the room. They did not see her again during their visit. Mrs Whelan and Nora Whelan brought them upstairs to have tea, and told them that Larry had not been in the house on Christmas Day. A few days later, Patrick Whelan called to see Mrs Griffin at home in Kilmacthomas. She had met him only once before, three years earlier. He told her that 'poor Larry is gone to heaven' and that she would 'have to make the best of it'. He then said, bizarrely, that if the gardaí finished searching the bog, he would organise a party to search it again, but that if he was to search it now and he found the body, the gardaí would say he himself had dumped the body there in the first place! The Whelans were clearly feeling the finger of suspicion pointing towards them. Patrick Whelan also lied to Mrs Griffin, telling her that there had been no visitors – let alone her husband – in his house on Christmas Day. The bad faith shown by the publican towards the distressed wife of the missing postman casts serious doubt over the sincerity of his motivation in calling on her at this time.

The claim by the Whelan family that no drink had been served on the premises on Christmas Day was now exposed beyond any shadow of doubt as a blatant lie. Jack Galvin, a farmer who lived a few miles inland from Stradbally at Fox's Castle, admitted that he had gone to Whelan's with another local man, Ed Dunphy of Carrigahilla, at about 7.30 p.m.:

> I think we had five or six bottles of stout apiece. We were at the kitchen fire. Patrick and Mrs Whelan, his son James and his two daughters Cissie and Norah [sic] and his other two young sons were there. I saw Guard Frawley there. He came into the kitchen at about 9.00 p.m. or 9.30 p.m. … He had no drink in our presence. He was sober. I think he was only after coming from cycling with the sergeant … Guard Frawley left after about ten minutes. I don't say he left the premises but he went out in the yard to my knowledge. He did not appear to have any drink taken, but may have had drink taken for all I know. I didn't see anyone else, but I thought I heard a voice like William Cleary's of the Cove Stradbally. I think he was with Guard Frawley. The piano was played while I was there, in the next room. We left there at about 11.00 p.m.

Ed Dunphy added that it was Nora who played the piano in

the parlour. Neither man saw Larry Griffin but they had come straight into the kitchen through the back door, and had not been in the pub section of the house. Ed Dunphy told the gardaí that the postman could have been in the house without his knowledge.

Both men said that Cissie Whelan had been in Whelan's while they were there. But both Cissie and Garda Dullea had claimed that they had strolled to Stradbally Cove together that night. The witnesses at Whelan's corner had already said that this could not have happened as described, and now here were further witnesses saying Cissie had been in Whelan's. The courting couple came up with a new story but they couldn't even get their facts straight about this one. Cissie said that they had been together in an outhouse behind Whelan's pub from about 7 p.m. until 10 p.m., and that they had lied about this because they didn't want Cissie's parents to know what they'd been up to! Cissie claimed that she had gone into the house several times during the course of the night so that she wouldn't be missed by her mother. In an era with a much more restrictive sexual morality than today's, this was an excuse for lying that had a ring of truth about it. The problem was that, while Dullea told a similar story, he said that they had been hiding out in the old ruins on the other side of the Chapel Road, rather than in Whelan's outhouse. The new story was clearly no more truthful than the old one.

Meanwhile, Fr O'Shea in Ballylaneen had persisted in his

own enquiries about the postman's disappearance. His house was beside the school in which Thomas Cashin and his wife taught, and as he knew that they lived in Stradbally village he often discussed the case with them. According to Chief Superintendent O'Mara's account, on about 22 January Mrs Cashin said to Fr O'Shea 'that the Guards would never find out what happened' regarding the postman and she gave him to understand that her husband had been present at whatever had happened. Furthermore, Cashin himself had later said to Fr O'Shea that 'the guards would never succeed in implicating him, or words to that effect'.

Remarkably, Cashin wasn't brought in for questioning. According to O'Mara's account, he and Superintendent Meehan had intended to bring Cashin in immediately, but he was away that particular evening. They then decided to question a local labourer, twenty-five-year-old Thomas Corbett, because Meehan had information that he knew something about the case. According to Chief Superintendent O'Mara's account, when Thomas Corbett came to the station, another man who became a key figure in the missing postman story came with him: this was Jim Fitzgerald, a fifty-year-old bachelor, known locally by his mother's surname of Greaney. Fitzgerald/Greaney was a stout man, with dark hair beginning to turn grey, a moustache and a sallow complexion. When Thomas Corbett's girlfriend Bridget had become pregnant with his child, thus forcing them into a speedy marriage, Fitzgerald had taken pity on them and taken them into his own house at Knockhouse, about a quarter of a mile from the village.

As Superintendent Meehan began taking a statement from Thomas Corbett, Chief Superintendent O'Mara started chatting with Fitzgerald in a separate room and after a while Fitzgerald, of his own accord, gave the statement that would turn the missing postman case into an international sensation. Or at least that was O'Mara's version of what happened, but comments later made by Corbett's wife and by Fitzgerald suggest that, far from wandering into the garda barracks and giving a statement of his own accord, Fitzgerald was deliberately taken in for questioning along with Corbett. The circumstances under which Fitzgerald gave his statement are of crucial importance, and later became a matter of great controversy.

Statement of James Fitzgerald (Greaney, Knockhouse, Stradbally on 23 January 1930)

I remember Xmas Day, 1929. I left my home at about 6.00 p.m. Tommy Corbett lives with me. Both of us came into the street and we stopped at Whelan's corner at about 6.30 p.m. Jim Murphy happened to come to Whelan's corner as we were coming across the village. The three of us stood talking at the corner. Patrick Cunningham came to the corner afterwards and remained talking to us. Josie Stephens passed through the street on his way home from Matt Drohan's. He stopped a few minutes and went away.

We stayed standing at the corner until the two guards passed with the bicycles. We were there about a half an hour at that time. After the two guards passed we went in by the back gate to Whelans. We knew it was the sergeant and Guard Frawley had passed and as the sergeant was the only man we were afraid of we thought we were safe in going. I hadn't seen the sergeant before that, that night.

I went into Whelan's first. I lifted the latch on the kitchen door. Tommy Corbett and Patrick Cunningham and Jim Murphy followed me in. I saw Mrs Whelan and Mary (Jack) Hannigan in the kitchen. Mary had a pint and was sitting near the fire smoking a clay pipe. I called for four pints and Cissie brought them. Mrs Whelan told her as Cissie wasn't in the kitchen when we went in. I don't know where Cissie was. She may have been in the bar. We stood up in the kitchen. Mrs Whelan remarked that we need not be afraid as the sergeant and Guard Frawley were gone to Bunmahon. We heard singing in the sitting-room and the piano playing. Cunningham remarked that he knew who was singing. I heard him singing in the room after 'The Oul Stone Wall'. Cunningham stood us another pint each to Corbett, Murphy and I before he went into the room. He drank his own in the kitchen.

I didn't go into the room. I went out to the yard and I looked in through the room window. I saw Patty and George Cummins there. I saw Cissie Whelan sitting at the piano and Guard Dullea was standing near her and he was singing. I saw Nora Whelan sitting down and Guard Murphy who was in uniform was sitting near her. I saw Jack Galvin of Foxe's Castle. I saw Mike Corbett of Carrickbarahan. I didn't see Cunningham or Jim Murphy in the room. Tommy Corbett was in the kitchen this time.

I then came back into the kitchen. I heard noise in the bar – shouting and singing – but I didn't go to the bar. I heard Cissie come out of the room and pull across the slide of the bar and shout in to stop the noise or they'd be heard in the street. I then left the kitchen and came along towards the middle door. I saw her pull back the slide. I was standing at the door of the room where the piano was playing then. When she pulled back the slide I couldn't see who was in the bar. Cissie saw me at the door and she didn't say anything to me. I was standing in the hall waiting for a drink. I happened to see Cissie coming from the bar to the room and I ordered a drink from her. She went into the room and she came out again to tell them to stop noising. She brought me my bottle of stout before going into the room the first time.

As soon as I got my bottle of stout I went back to the kitchen. I saw Cissie drawing back the slide but I don't know where I saw her from. When I went out to the kitchen Corbett had a bottle of stout but I don't know where he got it or how.

While I was standing in the hall I saw a man coming out of the bar and going down towards the lavatory. I'd say he was very like Larry Griffin. He had a postman's cap on him. His back was towards me as he went down. He had the postbag on his back. There was nobody with him. I didn't see him going back. It wasn't

Curran. It was Larry Griffin. I think this was after I heard the row in the bar but I am not sure. I don't know whether he had the chin strap down or not.

Ned Morrissey was in the bar that night. William Cleary was in the bar and old Pat Whelan was in the bar and he wasn't sober. Jim Murphy was in the bar. Pat Cunningham was in the bar. I was in the bar. Tom Corbett was in the bar. Mr Cashin, NT [National Teacher] was at the corner with us and he was in the bar with us later on. John Cunningham (Grady) was in the bar. Patrick Cummins and George Cummins were in the house but I didn't see them in the bar.

Three half-crowns fell from the Postman and Ned Morrissey picked them up and stood a drink as far as it went. The Postman himself fell on his face and hands. He fell in the bar towards the door (street) and against the stove. He should be hurt. His forehead struck the stove and he bled some but not much. His forehead was split across the centre. After striking the stove he dropped to the ground. He never spoke after falling. Ned Morrissey turned him over on his back and he said get up but Larry made no answer. Pat Whelan said he was dead and he rushed from behind the bar. Nobody said anything about going for the priest or doctor.

Ned Morrissey and Larry had a few words about money. Larry raised the three half-crowns and he told Morrissey that he had it. Morrissey said he hadn't and he gave him a jostle and Larry fell. He put his leg in front of him and threw him over it. Morrissey is a bit of a boxer.

Whelan said to Morrissey: 'You have me ruined. You have killed the man in my house.' Everyone who was in the house came into the bar then. The two guards, the two Cummins, Jack Galvin, Ned Dunphy, Cissie and Nora and Jimmie and Paddy Whelan. When old Whelan attacked Morrissey and was abusing him Morrissey said "twill be all right we'll take away Larry and nobody will know anything about it'.

For taking away the body they used the master's motor car. The master himself drove the car. The body was taken out of the bar through the back gate. The body was wrapped in a white blanket. It was twisted around him. Ned Morrissey pulled the bag off him. Morrissey put the bag on himself and I'm sure he put the cap in the bag.

Morrissey and Mr Cashin, NT, George Cummins and Paddy Whelan carried him out and put him in the car. Nobody said an act of contrition in his ear. They put him into the back of the car. Mr Cashin drove the car himself. Ned Morrissey got into the car beside him in front. The car went up towards the chapel. Dullea took out Larry's bicycle and said he'd leave it out at the Five Cross Roads somewhere. Guard Murphy was with him and went with him.

I heard them talk of where they would go with the body. Morrissey and Cashin said they'd go to Kilmacthomas and down to the mine shaft at Bunmahon where they'd drop the body. They said they'd go through Kilmacthomas and down to the shaft. They said that the bridge at Kilmacthomas would be a good place to dump him over. I'd say myself they went to the mine holes. I'd say they went to the one in Tankardstown.

They went up the Chapel Road and after about an hour they came back by Newtown and Stradballymore. I wasn't in the village when the car came back but I heard how and when it came back. It was George Cummins told me. When they were going, they took a half hundred weight with them. It passed between them-selves before they left that they'd stop at Kilmacthomas Bridge in order to do away with him there and if they didn't think that all right that they'd go to Tankardstown. I didn't hear since where they put him. All the fellows that were in the house that night were laughing at the guards searching round here for Larry but I never heard where he was. They got the weight at Whelan's.

James Fitzgerald

Witnessed by H. O'Mara C/S
Patrick Sullivan, Gda 3321

Chapter 6

Nobody in Stradbally knew as yet about Jim Fitzgerald's extraordinary statement. All they knew was that the farm labourer had suddenly disappeared from the locality a month after the disappearance of the postman, further adding to the aura of mystery surrounding the case. However, the *Waterford Weekly Star* eventually found out from Fitzgerald's lodgers, the Corbetts, that he had been taken in for questioning by the gardaí, and had never returned home except for one visit in the middle of the night to collect some clothes. It was still not known where he was staying, and the fact that he was not under arrest further fuelled speculation and rumours.

In fact Fitzgerald was now an officially protected state witness at Lady Lane barracks in Waterford city. Chief Superintendent O'Mara wrote to General O'Duffy that, having given his statement, Fitzgerald had 'approached me at Stradbally and stated that because of the information given by him, he was afraid to leave Stradbally barracks and asked that he be allowed to remain with the garda'. O'Mara told the commissioner that he felt it was advisable 'in the interests of the man's safety and to prevent him being influenced in any way by, or on behalf of, the suspected persons, to allow him to remain under garda protection'. Permission to maintain Fitzgerald as a protected witness was granted by the Minister for Justice, James Fitzgerald-Kenny.

What Fitzgerald had alleged in his statement was an extraordinary conspiracy to cover up Larry Griffin's death and dispose of his body involving, to some degree, about twenty local people including such pillars of the community as a school principal, a publican and two members of An Garda Síochána. Apart from the publican's family, the others named by Fitzgerald were mostly farmers. Fifty-one-year-old Ned Morrissey, whom Fitzgerald was accusing of killing Larry, was the local gravedigger. However, at the time of the 1911 census he had been living under the Whelans' roof and was employed by them full-time as a labourer. It is clear that this was no longer the case in 1929 but it shows that Morrissey was closely connected to the Whelan family.

Fitzgerald's description of Larry Griffin's death was vivid, detailed and compelling. Chief Superintendent O'Mara was convinced of its veracity and yet, in the next room, Thomas Corbett, who had been with Fitzgerald on Christmas night, was telling a totally different story about the same event. This was made all the stranger by the fact that Corbett was a lodger in Fitzgerald's house and that both of them had walked to the barracks together. Corbett agreed that he and Fitzgerald had gone around to the back of Whelan's on Christmas night to see if they could gain entry, but that was as far as their accounts coincided:

> (Greaney) Jim Fitzgerald went to the kitchen and tried the door. He turned round then and said to me 'locked up'. We only remained in Whelan's back yard while (Greaney) Fitzgerald was knocking and then came out. We did not see Mrs Whelan and I did not see any light in the windows … A man by the name of Pat Cunningham did not go into Whelan's with us …

Corbett then gave a detailed account of his and Fitzgerald's movements for the rest of Christmas night, which did not involve being in Whelan's.

In an attempt to get at the truth the gardaí again called in Jim Murphy for questioning. Eighteen-year-old Murphy was employed as an assistant gardener in the nearby Woodhouse estate. He was one of the men who had been standing at Whelan's corner on Christmas night and who had already given evidence of seeing Garda Dullea with Larry Griffin passing round the corner. Fitzgerald had named Murphy as one of the men who had followed him into Whelan's by the back door. But now Murphy gave a third version of the story: he claimed that he, Corbett and Fitzgerald had neither tried to get into Whelan's nor even suggested it. The farmer, Patrick Cunningham, the third man Fitzgerald had said followed him into Whelan's, also denied that any attempt had been made to enter the pub.

Fitzgerald's evidence seemed to confirm Chief Superintendent O'Mara's suspicions about the involvement of local gardaí in the postman's disappearance. It was in keeping with the stories and hints that were being collected from Fr O'Shea and the local community. It also tallied with eyewitness testimony that the postman and Garda Dullea had entered Whelan's, and with the evidence that Patrick Whelan himself had said to the Kilmacthomas men on St Stephen's Day that Larry Griffin had been in the pub the night before. It seemed to make sense of Garda Dullea's attempt to cover up being with the postman on Christmas night and of the Whelans' denials that drink was served in the pub or that the postman was present. It is difficult to believe that a country labourer such as Fitzgerald could have concocted such a compelling statement entirely on his own.

On the other hand, none of the other potential witnesses Fitzgerald named supported his story. The men at the corner denied going into Whelan's with him. Of the other persons named by him as being present in Whelan's when the postman was killed, some had already given statements which contradicted Fitzgerald's and the others did so in the coming days. They either denied that they had been in Whelan's or, if they admitted being in the pub, they denied that Larry Griffin or Jim Fitzgerald had been there. Some had certainly lied in their original statements and had been forced to change their stories, but there were other possible motives for some of these lies. The Whelans could have been lying to cover up the fact that they had broken the law by serving drink on Christmas Day. And the Stradbally guards could have been lying to cover up various breaches of regulations such as drinking on duty and not carrying out patrols.

There were some contradictions in the evidence of those whose statements were stacked against Fitzgerald. If Fitzgerald was lying and they were all telling the truth, it would be expected that their statements would tally with each other. As we have already seen, Corbett claimed that an attempt had been made to enter Whelan's but Murphy and Cunningham contradicted this. Corbett and Murphy agreed that while they were standing at Whelan's corner they got four bottles of stout from Nora Whelan at the front door and drank them on the street, but Cunningham contradicted this. Corbett said that he and Cunningham went to another pub in the village, O'Reilly's, and spent some time drinking there, and that after that they went on to the village hall. However, Cunningham said they went straight from Whelan's corner to the hall. Some allowance must be made for the possibility of memory lapses and the effects of alcohol. As Cunningham himself said when pressed on the matter:

I don't think I was in Riley's [sic] public house that night. I was kind of muddled after whiskey that night and I admit it. I have not much doubt about it I have a very poor memory when I take much drink ... I did not see Nora Whelan that night outside Whelan's front door. I don't remember her bringing out four bottles of stout to us that night, but she may have done it.

On the other hand Cunningham's memory loss was suspiciously selective. While he accepted that he might have been in O'Reilly's pub and forgotten about it, he was adamant that he could not have been in Whelan's:

> When a number of people tell you that I had drink at Whelan's
> on that night they are telling lies. I may have [*sic*] a drink outside
> Whelan's I am not sure. The only thing that makes me think that
> I had drink outside Whelan's is because ye mentioned it to me.
> I know you have suggested to me that I was inside Whelan's. I
> know that I was not in Whelan's and the fact that you suggest it
> to me does not make me think I was inside ... If people say I was
> in Riley's [*sic*] they may not be telling lies but if they said I was in
> Whelan's they would be telling lies.

The part of Thomas Corbett's narrative of Christmas night that is hardest to dismiss, because of the amount of corroborating evidence from other witnesses, is his account of what happened in the village hall. Corbett and several other witnesses name many of the same men as being present in the hall that night playing cards. Then, according to Corbett, a fight started between himself and another local man, William Cleary, and here again the consistency in the statements of various witnesses is striking.

THOMAS CORBETT

We were not long playing when an argument started between myself and William Cleary. Jim Fitzgerald (Greaney) came between us. Cleary did not want to stop. Guard Frawley walked over from the door then and told us to stop before there would be more trouble about it.

WILLIAM CLEARY

I am sure we would be over an hour playing when a row started over the cards and the game was broken up. Tommy Corbett stood up to hit me when I got the cards under his legs on the floor. I understood that he intended to strike me. I stood up then and got a bit vexed and prepared to defend myself. Jim Fitzgerald or Jim Greaney as he is known, got up to prevent the row.

PATRICK CUNNINGHAM

There was an argument about cards between Corbett and William Cleary and Corbett invited Cleary out in the yard to fight. Greaney and I took Corbett home. I did not see any guard at the hall that night. A guard could be there unknown to me and I would not mind.

MIKE CORBETT

> Just before we stopped playing there was an argument between
> Clery [*sic*] and Corbett over the cards. During the argument
> Guard Frawley came in and stopped the argument.

If anything, the fact that Patrick Cunningham couldn't
remember Guard Frawley being present almost adds to the
credibility of these statements. Cunningham, as we have seen
before, was very drunk on the night in question and seemed to
have great difficulty recalling many aspects of it. The way the
two men involved in the fight blame each other has a ring of
truth about it. The evidence that Guard Frawley was present in
the hall contradicts Frawley's own account of his movements
that night, so this evidence certainly was not concocted as part
of a coordinated conspiracy with the local guards. And the fact
that this fight seems to have been remembered more clearly by
witnesses than other parts of the night also has a ring of truth
about it – it is the kind of event that would be remembered.
For all these reasons it is difficult to believe that this part of
Corbett's testimony could be anything other than the truth.
And if it is the truth, it places Fitzgerald, Cunningham and
Corbett in the hall, and not in Whelan's pub witnessing Larry
Griffin's death.

Could it be that Fitzgerald witnessed the death of Larry
Griffin in Whelan's and was present at the fight in the hall at
different times on the same night? This would mean that this

part of Corbett's statement is true but that other parts of it are not. Fitzgerald's statement does not say what he and the other men did after Larry's body was taken away, so they could in theory have gone to the hall. However, it is difficult to imagine the men, even with drink taken, sauntering over to the hall to play cards after witnessing the death of Larry Griffin and its subsequent cover-up. There is no evidence that the investigating officers put this point to Fitzgerald or that they even realised the serious problem the fight in the hall caused for the case they were developing. A good defence barrister would not have overlooked such strong alibi evidence. The guards, however, were so convinced of Fitzgerald's credibility as a witness that, even though they had no body and virtually no corroborating evidence, they decided they had a strong enough case to proceed with charges and arrests.

Chapter 7

MURDER CHARGE

SENSATION IN
CO. WATERFORD MYSTERY

MISSING POSTMAN

ARREST OF TEACHER
AND LABOURER

(*Irish Independent* headlines, 25 January 1930)

Early on the morning of 24 January Garda Superintendent Meehan and two garda sergeants went to the house of the school principal Thomas Cashin to arrest him. When Superintendent Meehan knocked on the door Cashin stuck his head out his bedroom window upstairs and called out: 'Who is there? Guards?'

'Yes. Open the door,' ordered Meehan. Cashin came downstairs in his bare feet with only his trousers and shirt on. Meehan told him to put on his clothes and, as Cashin went back upstairs, Sergeant Thomas Murphy followed him. While Cashin entered the bedroom where his wife and child were in bed, Sergeant Murphy stood at the door. Mrs Cashin asked her husband: 'What's up now?'

Cashin replied: 'I don't know. They want me at the barracks.'

Mrs Cashin then made the cryptic remark in Irish: 'An fear mór marbh' ('the big dead man' or perhaps 'the dead important man').

Ned Morrissey was also taken from his home to Stradbally garda station that morning and both men were driven to Waterford district court where they were charged as follows:

1. that they and each of them did on 25 December 1929, at Stradbally, unlawfully and feloniously murder one Laurence Griffin;

2. that they and each of them did at the same time and place secretly dispose of the dead body of the said Laurence Griffin with intent to obstruct and prevent a coroner's inquest;

3. that at the same time and place they did steal, take and carry away a postbag and a postman's cap, value £5, the property of the postmaster general.

Cashin denied the charges. In reply to the first two charges

Morrissey said: 'The only thing I have to say is that I was not out since 4 o'clock that evening.' On being charged with the larceny, he said: 'Gorra, that's funny sir.' On being informed by Superintendent Meehan that every facility would be given them to consult a solicitor, Cashin said: 'I won't do anything for the present. There is plenty of time.' Morrissey enquired if it would be any use to bring a certificate of character from the nuns at the convent in Stradbally, where he was employed for twenty-six years. Superintendent Meehan told him this was not necessary at that stage.

Superintendent Meehan then had the men brought to a special district court sitting in Waterford where they were formally charged. As the defendants had no legal representation at this hearing, District Justice Mr F. J. McCabe advised them not to say anything. Cashin asked the judge if he would allow bail but this request was refused due to the seriousness of the charges. Having heard evidence of the arrests, the district justice informed each of the accused that they were entitled to ask the superintendent any question they wished. Morrissey said: 'I have nothing to ask. I was not there. I had nothing at all to do with the transaction.' Note the implication in Morrissey's words that the alleged event did in fact happen, just that he wasn't present himself. Cashin said: 'No. I will ask no questions just now.' The judge then remanded the accused in custody to appear in front of the court again in a week's time. He told the accused that in the meantime they could get into communication with their friends or employ a solicitor and that they would be given every facility. Cashin said: 'That's all right sir.' Morrissey said nothing and the proceedings came to an end. The two men were then brought to Ballybricken prison in Waterford.

Strangely, the gardaí never took a statement from Thomas Cashin about his movements on Christmas Day, either before or after he was charged. This is all the more remarkable when one considers that Cashin owned the only motor car in the village in which, according to Jim Fitzgerald's statement, Larry Griffin's body had been taken away. A senior guard later tried to justify this failure by claiming that 'the officers who were then investigating the case knew it would be a waste of time to seek an interview with him and that anything he would tell would be misleading'.

Cashin's wife, however, was questioned a few days after his arrest about his movements on Christmas Day. She said that when she was preparing the Christmas dinner in the early afternoon her husband went out of the house for a while. Mrs Cashin said she knew he was not in Whelan's pub at that time because 'he never goes to any public house on Sundays during prohibited hours as he has his position to mind and besides the young Whelans slip it out to him anytime he could not legally go in for it'. She also said that he was afraid to go into Whelan's because 'Sergeant Cullinane was very strict'. This doesn't sound very like the Sergeant Cullinane who tolerated numerous breaches of regulations by his own guards, including drinking in the barracks, and who allowed the guards to accept liquor from a local publican.

Larry Griffin had called to the Cashin house with the mail at about 2.30 p.m. and according to Mrs Cashin he had nothing to eat or drink in the house. She then said that at about 3 p.m. her husband, herself, three of their children and Garda Murphy travelled from Stradbally to the neighbouring village of Bally-laneen in the family car, on a pious mission – to put up a new holy statue in Ballylaneen chapel. A Ballylaneen woman, Miss Margaret Brett, confirmed this. She said that Mr Cashin and Garda Murphy called in to her to borrow a brush to sweep the chapel, and that Cashin drank a bottle of stout and Murphy, who was in uniform, had a glass of port. Mrs Cashin said that they got back to Stradbally at about 4.15 p.m. and that Garda Murphy had tea with them. Murphy then left for the barracks. However, Garda Murphy never mentioned this outing in his account of Christmas Day. According to Murphy, he was lying on his bed between 3 p.m. and 5 p.m., sleeping for some of the time and reading about crime the rest of the time in a publication called *World's Pictorial*.

Mrs Cashin said that Paddy Whelan the publican visited them between about 6.15 p.m. and 6.55 p.m. She made sure to mention that she and her husband said the rosary after the publican left, thus further emphasising the Cashins' pious credentials. She gave an account of her husband's movements that had him hanging around the house all evening and definitely not going to Whelan's pub. She said they both went to bed together at 10.15 p.m. The next morning around midday she said her husband came into the house and said to her:

> My God there is something serious about Larry. He has not returned yet and they are searching the bogs for him. I had better bring out a few of the lads and drop them along the road to look for him and see where he is.

Mrs Cashin also gave an interview to one of the newspapers, protesting her husband's innocence:

> An 'Examiner' representative interviewed Mrs Cashin, wife of the arrested national teacher, arriving at her home … in a pony and trap. Mrs Cashin is also a teacher, and she was just then getting back after her day's duties at Ballylaneen schoolhouse, some four or five miles away, where she and her husband teach. With her in the trap was a driver and those of her seven young children who are of school-going age.

In the course of the interview, which was given 'very willingly' by Mrs Cashin, she told the reporter that her husband had a perfect answer to the terrible charge made against him:

> She had no doubts whatever as to his absolute innocence in the

whole dreadful affair, and with his conscience clear, as he had assured her when she visited him in the Waterford prison, her husband had no fear of any investigations that might be made …

Mrs Cashin obviously made a good impression on the journalist who wrote that she was 'bearing the burden of this strain with wonderful fortitude' and that her 'ardent hope, and that of her husband, is that sufficient evidence will be forthcoming as will lead to his speedy release and the restoration of happiness to their little family circle'.

However, Department of Education documents reveal a rather less flattering portrait of Mr and Mrs Cashin. For the previous four years Thomas Cashin's work as a teacher had been rated non-efficient in inspectors' reports. He had no Irish-language qualification and in each of the years 1924, 1925 and 1926 he had failed in the examination for a certificate in Irish. He didn't turn up for the exam in 1927, failed it again in 1928, and didn't turn up for it in 1929. In May 1928, after many warnings about the standard of his work, he was told that 'serious action' would be taken against him if matters did not improve. However, even this ultimatum did not have the desired effect, as an extraordinary report of an inspection visit to the school on 20 July 1928 reveals:

The principal teacher, Mr Cashin, arrived at 11.55 a.m. official time. Mr Cashin stated that the school was keeping the 'Old

Time' by which reckoning he was one hour and twenty-five minutes late.

The assistant, Mrs Cashin, was absent. Mr Cashin refused to give any reason for her non-appearance.

Twenty-five pupils were obliged to sit on the roadside from the time I arrived – and before – till 12 o'clock.

The Principal's excuse for the foregoing state of affairs was that he 'notified Mr O'Connell, inspector, early in the week that the school was being closed on Friday, 20 July'. He further added to me that 'the pupils … came for the purpose of tidying up the School', and that he 'had not intended to proceed with official work that day'.

Mr Cashin then ordered two boys to clean the windows, as if to confirm his statement, as given above.

The facts, that the infant pupils were present, that all pupils had books and lunch, that it is an unusual proceeding for a teacher to get the windows cleaned in a school about to be closed for five or six weeks, not to speak of Mr Cashin's general demeanour, convinced me that this Teacher was not speaking the truth, and led me to form the opinion that had I not been there, the attendance would have been duly recorded as an official school day.

I may further add that Mr Cashin's manner and speech were rude and defiant in the extreme.

When asked to specify how Cashin had been rude and defiant, the inspector elaborated that the teacher's speech had been 'in the loud, angry, defiant tone usually adopted by a bully when discovered in the wrong'.

Even before the disappearance of Larry Griffin, Thomas Cashin was walking on thin ice as regards his tenure at Bally-laneen National School. He told a local man, George Crowley, sometime before Christmas 1929 that he was afraid he had lost the school. Even if he had not been directly involved in the postman's death, his very presence at an illegal drinking session where a man had been killed would have sealed his fate. The loss of social and economic status this would have entailed gave him a strong enough motive to cover up such a death, and to use his position of leadership in the community to induce others to keep their silence.

Jim Fitzgerald by contrast was a labourer, a man of no great social standing, who had put himself in a most stressful and lonely position. He alone was coming forward to accuse some of the most powerful and prominent members of his own small community – men like Thomas Cashin – of a terrible crime.

Meanwhile, most of the Whelan family were again brought in for questioning. Mrs Bridget Whelan now admitted that certain people had been drinking on the premises at various times on Christmas Day, either in the kitchen or in the parlour, including Ed Dunphy and Jack Galvin, who had themselves admitted being there. However, she denied that anyone had been in the pub, and denied that most of the people Jim Fitzgerald had named were present on the premises. Neither

Jim Murphy nor Ned Morrissey had been there, she insisted, nor had William Cleary, Pat Cunningham, Thomas Cashin, Jim Fitzgerald, Garda Dullea, Garda Murphy or, of course, the postman Larry Griffin. All the Whelans now stuck doggedly to this version of events in the pub on Christmas night.

Interestingly, however, Mrs Whelan continued to insist that her young unmarried daughter Cissie could not have been outside the house with Garda Dullea on Christmas night:

> Neither of my daughters was outside that night. Cissie did not and could not have spent any time outside the house that night. She could not have been outside for three hours or one hour or half an hour. I saw her continually in the house that night. If Cissie says she spent several hours outside the house that night with a guard it is a lie.

Cissie herself continued to insist that she had been with Dullea, not in Whelan's outhouse as she had earlier said, but in the ruins on the Chapel Road:

> I met him about 7 o'clock. We remained there about three hours or a little more. I left the ruins about five or six times while I was there with Guard Dullea for the purpose of letting my mother see me and letting her know I was in the house. I used the back way when entering my own house that night on each occasion when I left Guard Dullea … I played the piano a few times

during the times I was in and out to see Guard Dullea. I left
Dullea waiting in the ruins while I played the piano.

Because of Cissie and Garda Dullea's failure to get their facts
straight the first time they told this story, it was clearly a lie to
provide an alibi of some sort for Dullea. If this lie was indeed part
of the cover-up of Larry's death as Jim Fitzgerald had described
it, it would have been in Mrs Whelan's interest to concede that
her daughter could, after all, have been with Garda Dullea in the
ruins, as this would undermine Jim Fitzgerald's whole story. But
to admit that her young unmarried daughter had spent several
hours cavorting in an out-of-the-way place with Garda Dullea
would have been unthinkable to a woman like Mrs Whelan.
We know for certain that Mrs Whelan was lying to the gardaí
about the events of Christmas night. We know that she was
at the very least consciously hampering their investigation into
the disappearance of Larry Griffin, and that she was possibly
actively involved in that disappearance. These actions did not
seem to offend her sense of morality or respectability. But sexual
impropriety was obviously a different matter.

The Whelans were allowed to return home after this new
round of questioning, but that night they were visited by a
garda and a detective garda who had come to collect forensic
evidence. The two gardaí tried to remove the stove in the bar
off which Fitzgerald had alleged the postman had hit his head
when he fell, but they found that it was held fast to the wall.

They asked Nora Whelan if the family possessed an iron bar but she tried to discourage them from removing the stove, telling them there were no bloodstains on it. However, the gardaí had their orders and they managed to find an iron bar and to remove the stove from the wall. When they had done this they found a pair of lady's black stockings, which seemed to be bloodstained, concealed in a hole in the wall over the stove. They also found a coal scuttle which looked as if it was bloodstained. In addition, they removed an item of furniture that would have been known as a 'form' (pronounced locally 'furrum') – a long wooden bench or stool commonly found in country pubs. As they were trying to remove it, Cissie Whelan told them that there were no bloodstains on it and to leave it where it was. They ignored her comments, and both form and stove were brought back to the barracks.

The next day, Sunday 26 January, the publican Patrick Whelan was arrested, along with two others named in Fitzgerald's statement: George Cummins and Patrick Cunningham. When brought before District Justice McCabe in Waterford, none of the three made any statement and they were remanded in custody. Both men had previously denied being in Whelan's on Christmas night. However, when Patrick Cunningham's brother John heard that he had been arrested, he came to the station and made the following statement:

I am a brother of Patrick Cunningham who has been arrested

in connection with the disappearance of Laurence Griffin on 25 December 1929. I understand that he has denied being in Whelan's public house that night. I understand that he was somewhere on Whelan's premises that night with others and that he was served with drink there. I have reason to believe that he was there but that he had nothing to do with the disappearance of Larry Griffin. I would be glad to get an interview with him in order to influence him to admit all that he knows concerning what happened at Whelan's Public House on that night.

There is no record of whether John was allowed to talk to his brother but, if he did, he does not seem to have influenced him to change his story.

The gardaí returned to Whelan's looking for more forensic evidence. They removed six apparently bloodstained floorboards from the bar-room floor. On searching Mr and Mrs Whelan's bedroom, they found a lady's stocking which seemed to be almost completely covered in blood, concealed behind a wardrobe. In a drawer of the same wardrobe they found a portion of a blanket also smeared with blood and in the same drawer they found a piece of calico, a type of material made from cotton, which also appeared to be bloodstained. When they asked Cissie Whelan how she accounted for the presence of blood on the articles, she said: 'I don't know. I wish you would return them to me.' However, Mrs Whelan told one of the guards that the bloodstained items belonged to Cissie.

One of the gardaí found a coat belonging to Mr Whelan, which was hanging in his bedroom and which had stains resembling blood on it. On searching the inside pocket he found a number of letters and receipts. One of the receipts had two large bloodstains on it. He pointed out the stains on the paper to Cissie and asked her what she thought they were and she replied: 'I think it is blood, my father's finger might be cut.' However, the garda was of the opinion that the stains did not resemble finger marks but appeared as if the paper had come in contact with a cloth on which there was fresh blood.

The various stained items were brought back to the station and inspected by Superintendent Keenan. He then went to Whelan's himself to question Mrs Whelan and Cissie further about them. Cissie said that the bloodstained stocking and portion of blanket were related to her latest 'menstrual sickness', which had occurred in December. Why then, the superintendent asked, were they found in Mr and Mrs Whelan's bedroom? Mrs Whelan said that the room had been occupied by other members of the family for the first two nights since her husband's arrest. But that would not explain why Cissie would be bringing bloodstained clothes from her December period into her parents' bedroom in January, and hiding one of them behind a wardrobe. On the other hand, in the rural Ireland of 1930 this would have been an intensely embarrassing subject for daughter and mother to be forced to discuss with a male guard. Cissie's reluctance to be open and honest about the subject could be understood in this context. Furthermore, it is difficult to believe that the Whelans would keep pieces of cloth soaked with the postman's blood lying around the house, especially as the man of the house had already been arrested in connection with the alleged crime.

The gardaí returned to Whelan's again the following day and took away an apron, a man's shirt, a lady's dress and a piece of cloth which were all deemed to have suspicious stains on them. In the days following the various arrests they also seized many items of clothing from the houses of Ned Morrissey, Thomas Cashin and George Cummins. They also took away the teacher's motor car to conduct tests on blood-like stains in the car – a small stain on the under-edge of one of the doors and a large stain on the floor. Putting aside the articles which might be connected with the menstrual periods of the young Whelan women, it would be far more difficult to explain away the presence of human blood on items directly connected to the alleged killing and disposal of the postman's body.

All this activity naturally had quite an effect on the formerly quiet village of Stradbally. The *Cork Examiner* reported that a 'profound gloom' existed in the district: 'There is an anxious sullen look on every face. Silent and uncommunicative, every man regards his neighbour with distrust and all inform inquirers that they have no information.' A few days later, however, the same reporter wrote that 'startling stories' were in circulation regarding the mystery and that the local people 'ask eagerly for any scraps of information that may be picked up'.

Despite the arrests, the searches and the witness statements, the fact remained that this was still a murder case without an actual body. *The Irish Times* reported on 27 January 'that instructions had been received from General O'Duffy to the effect that the body must be found at all costs'. The bog near where the postman's bicycle had been found had previously been searched to no avail, but as a result of Fitzgerald's statement, the gardaí now had a new idea of where to look.

Chapter 8

A crowd of onlookers gathered around the abandoned Tankardstown mineshaft, near the village of Bunmahon, on a bitterly cold, windy and wet day near the end of January 1930. Copper mining had been a major industry around Bunmahon between 1827 and 1877. At its height, well over 1,200 people were employed in the mines, but as the quality of the ore being extracted gradually declined, the mines became commercially unviable and eventually closed. By now, Bunmahon and the surrounding area was a desolate landscape, pockmarked by abandoned mineshafts and ruined buildings, and almost totally denuded of its former population. There were no occupied houses in the vicinity of the Tankardstown shaft but the ruin of the old pumping engine house stood next to it.

About twenty yards away ran a narrow country road and, about thirty feet on the other side of that road, the coastal cliffs towered over a turbulent sea. The opening of the mineshaft had been covered by a strong wooden stage, with a special hatch in the middle of it, giving access to the shaft. As a uniformed garda stood guard on top of the stage, the foreman and other workmen were putting the finishing touches to the construction and making sure everything was secure.

The dangerous task of exploring the old mineshaft had been contracted out by the gardaí to a Waterford-based engineer, John Hearne. Mr Hearne himself was not present, but a reporter from the *Irish Independent* approached the foreman and engaged him in conversation, while the garda on duty did nothing to dissuade them. The foreman, Mr Reddy from Tramore, explained to the reporter that a cave-in had occurred in the shaft in 1906, and that it was blocked some 500 yards down. If the corpse was in the shaft it had to be resting on the stones, earth and timber which formed the stoppage. Mr Reddy then had the hatch removed and allowed the reporter to peer down into the shaft. 'No human eyes can pierce the density of the darkness a hundred feet below,' wrote the reporter in the next day's paper. Turning back to Mr Reddy he asked: 'When will it be investigated?'

'Not until we get a windlass and can lower a man in a boson's chair. We will probably do it tomorrow.'

'Standing over the pit,' wrote the reporter, 'it indeed seemed a suitable spot in which to hide a body on a dark night.' However, compared to some of the other mineshafts in the area, the Tankardstown shaft was a relatively straightforward one to search, because of the absence of water and because of the cave-in which would have stopped a body from falling too far. By the next morning it had been established that there was no corpse to be found there.

The focus now shifted to the Ballinasisla mineshaft, near the home of a Mrs Power, who had heard a motor car pull up with screeching brakes beside her cottage on Christmas night, keep its engine running for ten minutes and then depart again. The shaft itself was only three feet from the road, from which it was separated by a wall, itself only about three feet high. A senior officer in a telephone message to the Garda Commissioner General Eoin O'Duffy gave the opinion that 'if the car were pulled close to this wall it would hardly be necessary to leave it for the purpose of throwing the body down this shaft'. He also told General O'Duffy that 'it is most likely that the body was deposited in this shaft'. Arrangements were made for the dismantling of the stage over the Tankardstown shaft and for its re-erection at Ballinasisla. However, because the Ballinasisla shaft contained water, this was going to be a more complicated operation. The harbour master from Waterford was asked for advice on the best methods of getting up any objects that might be at the bottom. Having inspected the site he gave instructions for grappling hooks to be made up which could be lowered to the bottom of the shaft.

The case of the missing postman, as it had become known, was now making headlines in Ireland and Britain. The garda top brass were determined that they should be seen publicly to be doing everything possible to clear up the mystery. Perhaps with this in mind, one of the deputy commissioners of the force, Éamonn Coogan (father of the historian and former *Irish Press* editor Tim Pat Coogan) turned up in Waterford, accompanied by a group of correspondents from the various Irish and British newspapers. He told them, and they duly published in the next morning's papers, that he had taken charge of the case, much to the annoyance of Chief Superintendent O'Mara. The chief superintendent was also irritated by the presence of the reporters who, he said, 'became a nuisance and shadowed everybody engaged in the investigation'.

O'Mara accompanied the deputy commissioner to Ballina-sisla mineshaft but, as the grappling apparatus was not going to be ready until later that day, they went on to Stradbally. The normally quiet country village was now the centre of a major garda operation and there were more motor cars parked in the square than had ever been seen in the locality before. The deputy commissioner ordered that John Power be brought to the barracks again. Power was the sixteen-year-old witness who had made the first statement putting Garda Dullea in the postman's company on Christmas evening. When Power was brought to the station, O'Mara was out in the back yard talking to some of the guards involved in the investigation. In his account, written some years later, he then makes a most serious allegation against Deputy Commissioner Coogan:

> Detective Gardaí O'Rourke and Driscoll, who had brought young Power to the station … came out to the yard and were proceeding into an outhouse when I asked them where they

were going. They told me they were going to beat the truth out of Power on the deputy's instructions. I told them to let Power home and not to attempt to beat him. They complied with my order and let him go.

There was a certain tolerance of physical abuse of detainees and witnesses in the garda force in those early years. On the other hand, it is clear that there was no love lost between O'Mara and Coogan, and we do not have Coogan's version of the events at Stradbally. As we will see, O'Mara received much of the blame for what were later seen to be serious failures in the garda investigation of the missing postman case. His written account was an attempt to redress what he saw as an injustice done to him, and to place the blame firmly where he believed it to belong. At this remove, it is not possible to state for certain whether or not his allegations against Coogan are true. However, they do give us some insight into the personal enmities which existed within the garda force, a factor which cannot have helped the progress of the investigation.

According to O'Mara it was the deputy commissioner who ordered the next three arrests. The new detainees were Bridget Whelan, the wife of the publican Patrick who had already been arrested, their daughter Nora, and their son James. Cissie Whelan was never arrested and the garda files give no reason why not. This left only herself and her twelve-year-old brother at home. The new arrests brought the total of those in custody to eight, and only served to heighten further the press interest in the case. 'Sensation follows sensation with great rapidity as the situation develops in connection with the mysterious disappearance at Stradbally, County Waterford, of a postman named Laurence Griffin, who has been missing since Christmas Day,' reported the *Irish Independent* the next morning. The *Waterford Weekly Star* and the *Munster Express* carried the same description of the atmosphere in the village on the day of the latest arrests:

> From the half-closed doors and curtained windows of the shops and private residences surrounding the square in Stradbally, the residents could be seen watching with anxious interest the active operations of the Civic Guards and members of the detective force who now and then dashed off here and there in motor cars. Straight across the square is the home of Thomas Cashin the national teacher, who was one of the first to be charged with the crime. Outside it a Civic Guard paraded to and fro while, apparently unmindful of his presence, some of the younger children of the accused man played with their skipping ropes.

Having ordered the arrests, Deputy Commissioner Coogan and Chief Superintendent O'Mara returned to the Ballinasisla mineshaft where the dragging apparatus was now in working order. Coogan allowed the press reporters to join him at the edge of the shaft. A powerful electric lamp which could be lowered into the shaft had also been procured. As a large crowd of spectators looked on, the blaze of the light sank slowly into the darkness. The Ballinasisla shaft, being only ten feet in diameter, was narrower than the Tankardstown shaft which had been searched the day before. As the 1,000-candle power light was lowered, for the first hundred feet of the descent it lit up the sides of the shaft with great clearness. From throwing stones down the shaft and hearing them splash, the guards knew that the shaft contained water, but they hoped that it was just a few feet of stagnant rainwater. The *Waterford Weekly Star* reported what happened next:

> The light travelled down a big distance, to judge from the period of time expended in paying out the cable attached thereto. The deputy commissioner of the Civic Guards was amongst the little group on the platform who … sprawled full length over that deep shaft and strained their eyes to detect any evidence of a human body. The paying out process stopped, the gathering of fifty or sixty curious people on the roadway pressed closer to look over the fence wall and in through the space between it and the platform. A few minutes dead silence prevailed; then there followed a gentle whispering amongst the group of searchers. One thought he could discern something very like a body down below. Another held the view that only some rocks that jutted out from the sides of the shaft were visible, and others still believed they could make out other objects. All, however, were agreed on the point that below the light was running water.

Even those with field glasses could not say with any certainty what lay below, apart from the fact that there were flecks of foam on the water's surface. The motion of the water was bad news, for it suggested that the shaft was connected to the sea, which would make it more difficult to investigate properly. As well as the light, a long weighted rope had also been lowered to the bottom of the shaft to measure its depth. When it was hauled up it showed that the water level was 250 feet down and that the water itself went to a further depth of about 100 feet.

The dragging apparatus was now put to use, and the deputy commissioner stood at the ropes as the bodies of several pigs, goats and dogs were recovered on the hooks. As a result of local knowledge and their own observations, the engineering team and the guards began to realise that the search of the mineshaft was going to be far more problematic than had been first expected. There were subterranean galleries opening off the shaft in all directions. The fact that the water in the shaft was seen to rise and fall with the tide confirmed the suspicion that at least one of these galleries was connected to the sea. But as the sea was half a mile away as the crow flies, this underwater channel must be very extensive indeed. Even if no body was found in the shaft, it would not be conclusive proof that none had been thrown in, for the strength of the currents swirling at the bottom of the shaft could be sufficient to carry it away.

Meanwhile, Mrs Power began to have doubts about her story of a motor car pulling up to the edge of the shaft on

Christmas night. While she remained adamant that she had heard the car, she now thought that it might have happened two or three nights after Christmas night. As darkness fell at Ballinasisla, it was decided to halt operations for the night.

On the way back to Waterford city, Coogan and O'Mara stopped again at Stradbally garda station, where, according to O'Mara, the following bizarre incident happened:

> Detective Garda O'Rourke produced a blood stained garment which he found under or behind a press in Whelan's. He told how his search was due to a dream in which he had seen the blood stained article concealed in Whelan's.

Remarkably, Deputy Commissioner Coogan included the dream story in his official report to General Eoin O'Duffy. Neither Chief Superintendent O'Mara nor Deputy Commissioner Coogan passed any remark on this unorthodox investigation method, and simply noted it in their accounts as if it were just another normal part of the investigation. Detective O'Rourke also made an official report of the search of Whelan's which was inspired by his dream. On searching the top of a press in Nora Whelan's bedroom, he found a small apron and a piece of white cloth, both with bloodstains on them: 'I brought both articles under the notice of Cissie Whelan and asked her if she could account for the blood. She said "No" but she said the apron was the property of Nora her sister.' During

Detective O'Rourke's search an aunt of Cissie and Nora's was also present, as she was staying in the house to help out in the absence of the arrested family members. She was Mrs Galvin, the wife of Jack Galvin, who had admitted to being in the kitchen of Whelan's on Christmas night. As O'Rourke was searching, Mrs Galvin passed a remark:

> 'You know you will find things in relation to women here.' I asked her what did she mean by such a remark or did she know what I was looking for. She said 'I am not a fool and I needn't be a detective to know that.'

Detective James Driscoll also took part in this search of Whelan's and confiscated some items of clothing, including a dress belonging to Nora Whelan.

As a detective, O'Rourke was supposed to be part of a specially selected elite group of officers chosen for their intelligence and investigative abilities. Furthermore, as the commissioner himself had ordered that top priority should be given to this case, the gardaí had presumably sent their best men to Stradbally. And yet, even leaving aside the bizarre dream-based methodology, the whole episode smacks of amateurism and naivety. Remember, this was the third such visit to Whelan's, and by now several members of the family had been arrested. Either the house had been searched properly the first time or it hadn't. The Whelans were hardly likely to be hiding incriminating pieces of evidence around the house at this late stage. It was indeed inevitable that pieces of cloth stained with menstrual blood would be found among the personal possessions of young women such as Nora and Cissie Whelan in 1930. O'Rourke really was a 'fool' in regard to women's personal matters, as Mrs Galvin might have put it. He seemed to believe that he had found valuable pieces of evidence, and that Mrs Galvin's remarks were an effort to obstruct him, rather than a common-sense statement of the obvious. O'Rourke's weaknesses as an investigator were symptomatic of the haste with which the new garda force had been built up some years previously. He was only twenty-five years old, unmarried and clearly lacking in experience and knowledge of worldly affairs, let alone investigative methodologies. His only qualification to be a detective was that his father had been a sergeant in the Royal Irish Constabulary of pre-independence days, and indeed sons of former officers in that force did receive favourable consideration in recruitment to An Garda Síochána, such was the absence of recruits with any background in policing.

In spite of the arrests of several members of the Whelan household, the public house remained open for business with the help of Mrs Galvin. When the *Irish Independent*'s reporter visited Whelan's the same evening, Mrs Galvin said to him: 'Why shouldn't we keep the hotel open? The Whelans did nothing wrong and have nothing to be ashamed of. I don't believe they have any evidence against them. What could they have?' She also told the reporter that the Whelans and Larry Griffin were the best of friends, and that Larry was treated by them like one of the family.

Having heard the report of the latest search of Whelan's, Deputy Commissioner Coogan and Chief Superintendent O'Mara continued on to Waterford city, where the deputy commissioner again gave extraordinarily frank interviews to the press, much to their delight and to the further annoyance of Chief Superintendent O'Mara. Coogan admitted that the state's case depended on the discovery of the body and told the *Irish Independent* that, even if the body was in the Ballinasisla mineshaft, the gardaí might never find it due to the difficult conditions in the shaft. Coogan also complained 'that in this area the natural reticence of the Irish countryman was so strong that it was exceedingly difficult to get any information'. He was even more forthright in the confidential report he phoned in to General O'Duffy that night, as the garda files reveal: 'The whole countryside is in a conspiracy of silence. It is almost impossible to get any useful information. A number of those concerned have been pushed very far but without effect.' He also told O'Duffy that a Stradbally girl named Bridie Flynn, who was working in Dublin, knew a good deal of the facts of the case and that she had been in Whelan's on Christmas Day. He said that she 'should be interviewed and questioned very closely regarding the case'.

Bridie Flynn's family lived in the square in Stradbally and

she was a very close friend of the Whelan family, especially of Cissie. She had left Stradbally two days after Christmas Day to take up a position looking after the children of a well-off family in Castleknock, County Dublin. Ed Dunphy, who had admitted to being in Whelan's on Christmas Day, had actually said in his statement that he had seen her in the kitchen with Mrs Whelan. However, when she was interviewed by garda detectives in Dublin because of the assistant commissioner's report, she flatly denied that either she or any member of her family had been in Whelan's pub on Christmas Day or Christmas night. But Bridie Flynn's credibility as a witness is strained to breaking point by another part of her statement. She said that she did not hear that Larry had gone missing until the afternoon of St Stephen's Day, when she and her mother noticed the three Kilmacthomas men outside Whelan's enquiring about Larry Griffin.

> My mother was standing at our door with me, and Cissie Whelan was at the Hotel door. My mother called her and asked what was wrong and Cissie said that the men with the pony and trap were looking for Larry as he had not turned up at Kilmacthomas post office. She did not say anything about Larry being in the Hotel, or Hotel Bar, the previous night and neither I nor any member of my family had heard that anything unusual had occurred in Whelan's on Christmas Night.

We already know that both Patrick Whelan and Cissie Whelan told the Kilmacthomas group quite openly that Larry Griffin had been in the pub the night before. The notion that Cissie wandered over to Flynn's house at about the same time, and told them about the postman's disappearance while saying nothing about him being in the pub the night before, is not believable.

Bridie said that she left Stradbally for Dublin on 27 December and claimed that she had heard nothing further about the Larry Griffin story other than what she had read in the newspapers. Bridie had been gone from Stradbally for over a month when she was interviewed. Stradbally had been awash with rumours and stories about the fate of the missing postman. This was the biggest sensation to hit her home village in living memory. And yet she claimed that she hadn't had any communication with her family or anyone else in Stradbally about the matter. It is obvious that Ed Dunphy's evidence of Bridie being in Whelan's on Christmas Day was true, and that she was lying to protect her friend, Cissie, and the Whelan family.

Meanwhile, the prisoners were remanded in custody at Waterford courthouse on 31 January. After the hearing, one of the gardaí escorting the prisoners overheard Ned Morrissey's wife say to him: 'Remember Ned you have a tongue in your cheek and keep it there.' She also said to him that they were better off now than ever they were as the 'master's wife', meaning Mrs Cashin, was sending food and 'stuff' to the house. The Cashins clearly realised that Ned Morrissey, the poorest and least educated of the suspects, was the potential weak link in the conspiracy. They were going to make sure that he had a vested interest in maintaining solidarity with the more socially and economically powerful members of the group.

Chapter 9

By now the mystery of the missing postman had captured the imagination of the public. The Dungarvan correspondent of the *Waterford Weekly Star* wrote:

> The Stradbally mystery overshadows every other item of conversation in this place and district. Ever since the disappearance of Laurence Griffin became known inquiries have been made on every hand, and the wildest rumours imaginable have been circulated … The whole countryside is on tip-toe of expectation, and at any moment may be expected the news to come that the body of the poor postman has been found.

The Irish Times rarely strayed from straightforward reporting of the case, but the coverage in the *Irish Independent* captured the public fascination with it. Their correspondent predicted accurately that 'the mystery of the missing postman of Stradbally will be famous in the annals of Waterford for years to come'. He also identified the aspects of the case that would fascinate writers and the public, including me, down to the present day:

In many of its aspects this grim tale is unique, and in it life has presented materials for the writer of fiction if he had the imagination to conceive them. The very day of the disappearance heightens the sinister horror of the story.

On Christmas Day, the season of peace and good-will, a man visits a lonely village on the Irish coast. He is seen in the afternoon in the company of a number of men and women, and he is never seen again.

His bicycle is found some miles away the next day, but the man might have vanished into thin air for all the trace there is of him.

Having recounted in more detail the known facts about the postman's disappearance, the writer continued:

Now comes one of the strangest aspects of this remarkable case. Everyone knows the secretiveness of the Irish countryside, but surely the inhabitants of Stradbally surpass all other villages in this respect.

A man has vanished as if the earth had opened and swallowed him, a phrase grimly suggestive of the subsequent suspicion, and not a word is said.

Life goes on normally in the village, there is a brief paragraph in the newspapers, and then everything is quiet again.

The extraordinary thing that has happened is hardly realised by people outside the immediate locality, but in the neighbourhood every fireside has its whispering coterie.

This notion of the silent villagers concealing a terrible secret from the outside world was to remain a central motif of the story of the missing postman in the press, in folklore and in literary works which drew their inspiration from the case in subsequent decades.

On the morning of 30 January 1930, Deputy Commissioner Coogan returned to Dublin and directed Chief Superintendent O'Mara to accompany him. Before leaving Waterford he sent orders to HQ in Dublin to have the Stradbally garda party in his office at 5 p.m. By now they had all been moved to Dublin from their initial transfer destinations around the country and had been suspended from active duty. They were brought individually into the deputy commissioner's office to be interviewed, where, according to Chief Superintendent O'Mara's account written some years later, the following took place:

> The deputy commissioner questioned them, coaxed them, abused them and finally used a round ebony stick about two feet in length in such a cruel fashion that their yells could be heard not alone in the depot square but in the park. Gardaí Murphy and Frawley received particularly harsh treatment.

There is probably some truth to this account, because in later life Garda Sullivan told his own son, also a garda, that he had been beaten by senior officers during the investigation. The garda commissioner himself, General Eoin O'Duffy, personally interviewed Sergeant Cullinane of the Stradbally party and, according to O'Mara, 'the gardaí and I afterwards heard himself boast that he encouraged them with promotion if they told and threatened them with dismissal and charges of murder if they didn't tell the whereabouts of Griffin's body'. Whatever tactics were really used in the garda HQ interrogations, there was no breakthrough in the case. However, the gardaí from General Eoin O'Duffy down continued to be convinced that Gardaí Dullea and Murphy in particular knew more than they were telling.

Since being suspended from duty, the Stradbally gardaí had been confined to barracks and on half pay, causing particular difficulty for the families of Gardaí Sullivan and Frawley. Indeed, there seems to have been a deliberate strategy to make the women more vulnerable to pressure by isolating them from their husbands. As well as the physical separation, Frawley and Sullivan were not even allowed to write home for the first few weeks of their confinement to the depot. And, of course, their wives' letters to them were being intercepted and read. Senior gardaí impressed upon the women the seriousness of their husbands' situation and the women seemed most anxious to cooperate with the investigation into Larry Griffin's disappearance. Neither of them believed that their husbands were directly involved in the postman's presumed death but they thought that their husbands might not be telling all they knew out of a sense of loyalty to their colleagues. Without consulting her husband, Mrs Frawley decided to break ranks with Garda Dullea, and made the following statement to the investigating officers:

> I remember the 7 January 1930. Between 7.00 p.m. and 8.00 p.m. Guard Dullea called to my house. My husband was in bed sick and when Guard Dullea came up to the kitchen he seemed excited and he asked me could he see himself meaning my husband. I brought Guard Dullea to the bedroom where my husband was and then Guard Dullea asked me to go down and lock the door as he was afraid some of the officers would come over and catch him inside with Paddy. I barred the door as Dullea had told me and he remained talking with Paddy for about ten minutes. He left then and I opened the door for him. When he was going away he said to me 'Don't mention that you saw Larry and myself together on Christmas Day' or 'Don't mention that Larry and myself were in here on Christmas Day'. I asked him what it was all about and he said not to worry about it and that it was nothing. I knew there was something unusual going on in the barracks on the 7/1/30 and I guessed it was some enquiry about Larry Griffin.

There was indeed an unusual amount of activity going on in Stradbally barracks on 7 January for that was the date on which John Power first stated that he saw Garda Dullea in company with Larry Griffin on Christmas Day.

Both Mrs Frawley and Mrs Sullivan urged their husbands to tell all they knew. On 31 January Mrs Sullivan wrote to her husband:

> Indeed it has been 11 weary and trying days for us all. Just trusting in the Sacred Heart for the better. I was to Fr Burke. Just admit truth and you are clear … Superintendent O'Shea came to the house and told me to write and make you admit the truth … As Superintendent Meehan, Chief Superintendent O'Mara and commissioner told me, your job is in your hands to tell the truth and have a future to look to a wife and kids … The commissioner told me if Dullea tell truth [*sic*] he is free so for God's sake tell him to admit every twist and turn he gave and where he was that day also Murphy. So Jack, for love of the Sacred Heart, admit truth, my heart is scourged …

At the bottom of the letter there was a poignant message from one of the children: 'tell truth dada. Jim'.

Having received his wife's letter, Garda John Sullivan gave a statement in which he admitted to gross neglect of duty on his own part, and in which he revealed much more about the activities of the Stradbally guards on Christmas Day. We saw earlier that the Stradbally guards were contradicting each other over whether or not any alcohol had been consumed by them in the barracks on Christmas Day. While having a drink or two in the barracks on Christmas Day would have been a breach of regulations, it was a widespread practice and would not have had very serious consequences for the guards' careers. In a situation where a man was missing and suspected murdered, it was difficult to understand why innocent men would not simply tell the truth about such a relatively minor infringement. As Garda Sullivan now finally admitted, the answer to this mystery was that there was a lot more than a few drinks consumed in the barracks that day. The picture he painted was of a garda contingent totally lacking in discipline or order.

Chapter 10

Statement of Garda John J. Sullivan, 1 February 1930

I remember Christmas day 1929. I was barrack orderly at Strad-bally Station on that day. I was paraded by the sergeant. Having been paraded Garda Frawley was in the barracks and he asked me over to his house. This would have been about 10 a.m. Both of us went to Guard Frawley's and we had some drink – whiskey and stout. We stayed there for half or three-quarters of an hour and we went back to the barracks and the sergeant was there when we went in. We had a drink of whiskey in the barracks. The three of us then went down to my house. We had some whiskey and stout there again. Frawley and I then went over to Whelan's and the sergeant remained in my place. That would be after last mass. We met Patrick Cunningham at Whelan's corner. The three of us went in the back and we had either two or three drinks (bottles of stout) there. We didn't remain long and we went out the back again and down to Riley's [*sic*]. I think we had three stouts in Riley's. Frawley and I then went to the barracks. It would be about 2 p.m. then and I went down to my dinner at my own house. When I went in my dinner was ready. The sergeant was there. After my dinner I went back to the barracks and Frawley and I went to Whelan's again and from there to Riley's. We both went from Riley's back to the barracks again. It would then be somewhere about 4 p.m.

Garda Sullivan then admitted that he had basically spent the rest of Christmas Day and night sleeping off the effects of his drinking binge. He awoke to hear Gardaí Dullea and Murphy return to the barracks at 12.30 a.m. He admitted that he did not carry out any of his duties at all on Christmas Day, and that all of the entries in the station diary were concocted and entered the next day to give a false semblance of order.

Sullivan was now saying that Garda Dullea was not back in the barracks at 10.30 p.m. as he had earlier claimed and that Garda Murphy did not stay in the barracks after 9.30 p.m., but returned at 12.30 p.m. with Garda Dullea. It is therefore quite credible that Gardaí Dullea and Murphy had been drinking in Whelan's at the time Larry Griffin was alleged to have died, just as Gardaí Sullivan and Frawley had been drinking there earlier in the day.

Garda Sullivan's statement also helps explain why he, the sergeant and perhaps Garda Frawley had been lying through their teeth before this, even though they personally may have had nothing to do with Larry Griffin's death and disappearance. It is clear that there were much more than just minor infringements of regulations going on in Stradbally barracks. Discipline had totally broken down, and the station party from the sergeant down were in dereliction of duty. Sullivan, Frawley and the sergeant had more than enough reason to fear for their jobs and their livelihoods, and more than enough motivation to lie about their activities on Christmas Day. Even though they must have suspected that Gardaí Dullea and Murphy were involved in the postman's disappearance, they covered up for them at first on the basis that, if they didn't stand together, they would all fall together. However, Garda Sullivan began to realise that his days in the force were numbered, no matter what he did. He wrote to his wife:

I am sure this will soon be finished now but Bridie I think I will come out at the worst side, but I have one thing to be thankful for. I am or will be leaving with a clear conscience and we must trust in the Sacred Heart to keep us from starvation.

Chapter 11

After the interrogations at headquarters, General O'Duffy remained convinced of the guilt of Gardaí Murphy and Dullea and he ordered their arrest in connection with the postman's disappearance. They were arrested two days later and brought back to Waterford city to be charged and imprisoned along with the other suspects. On the journey back to Waterford, while conversing with one of his garda escorts, Garda Murphy said: 'Let them find the body. They can only remand me three times without taking depositions and then they must either return me for trial on bail or in custody or else refuse informations.' To 'refuse informations' meant to throw out the case against the accused. In other words, Garda Murphy was confident that there would not be enough evidence to return him for trial.

General O'Duffy also decided that he would travel incognito to Waterford to meet the local prelate Bishop Hackett, and he sent O'Mara back to Waterford ahead of him to make the appointment with the bishop. General O'Duffy arrived in Waterford on Sunday 1 February and he met the bishop at his residence. According to O'Mara's account, the bishop received General O'Duffy courteously, but refused his request to go on a special visit to Stradbally to exhort the congregation to come forward and assist the investigation. O'Mara wrote that he heard the commissioner saying later that night that Bishop Hackett was known in government circles as 'the weak man of the hierarchy'.

The following morning O'Duffy and Chief Superintendent O'Mara called to see Fr O'Shea at Ballylaneen and the priest told them whatever he knew about the case. From there they went to Stradbally barracks where O'Duffy expressed himself so highly satisfied with the investigations that he promised at least one man – Garda Twamley – promotion to the rank of sergeant.

Their next call was to Stradbally convent and while they were waiting for the reverend mother an old nun came to the side door of the reception room 'in a flurry', as O'Mara put it, and asked to speak to General O'Duffy. She told the commissioner that Tommy Corbett knew everything that had happened and that if the guards were to 'get after him' he would tell what he knew. Corbett was the man who had accompanied the chief witness Jim Fitzgerald to the garda barracks, when the latter had made his statement about the postman's death, and he also lived in Fitzgerald's house. Fitzgerald had named him as one of the men who had accompanied him into Whelan's pub by the back door, but Corbett had denied this. When the reverend mother came she told the commissioner that the nuns had heard digging either in the convent grounds or in the adjacent graveyard at some unearthly hour one night, the implication being that somebody had been either burying or disinterring a body. Having concluded with the nuns, the commissioner's party paid a courtesy visit to the elderly parish priest, Fr Lannon, 'who wouldn't believe that any human would injure poor Larry Griffin'.

On their arrival back in Waterford, General O'Duffy sent for the newspaper correspondents and informed them of the arrests of Gardaí Murphy and Dullea, which caused a great sensation in the following morning's newspapers. O'Duffy gave a special interview to the *Daily Mail* and *Daily Express* correspondents, in which he gave a history of the force from its inception and boasted about the number of officers who had the highest degrees in law. He said that he had visited Stradbally and found that the clergy in particular and the people generally were very helpful. Asked about the 'wall of silence', he said that it never existed and that any statement to that effect was incorrect. Another statement which had appeared in the press and which he wished to have contradicted was that headquarters' officers were in charge of the case. He emphasised that the local officers were in charge and that he had confidence in them.

The next day, 4 February 1930, all the men engaged in the investigations met General O'Duffy in conference from 9.30 a.m. to 1 p.m. Towards the end of the meeting Garda Inspector

Patrick McNamara arrived from Cork. The inspector had been summoned to assist in the investigation; since he had previously been based in Waterford, he knew the district and the people well, and he was highly regarded within the force. However, his actions during the course of the investigation were to prove highly controversial.

O'Mara's hopes of a breakthrough were raised by a new lead. His friend Fr O'Shea in Ballylaneen told O'Mara that a man by the name of Dennis Hannigan, known locally as Sonny, had been present in Whelan's public house when the postman was killed, and that he was accompanied by his uncle Morris 'who ran away home when he saw the blood'. Sonny Hannigan was an accountant at the National Bank at Bagnelstown, County Carlow, and one of his sisters was the postmistress in Stradbally. Because of this information O'Mara returned to Stradbally where he interviewed Sonny's sisters and 'they admitted, for the first time, that their brother was in Stradbally on the night of Griffin's disappearance and that he did go into Whelan's'. O'Mara went on to question their uncle Morris 'who protested vehemently that he wasn't in Whelan's and that he saw no row'. The chief superintendent then sent officers to Bagnelstown to interview Sonny Hannigan, who admitted to having been in Whelan's. However, hopes of a breakthrough were once again dashed when Hannigan denied seeing either the postman or any of the chief witnesses in the public house:

I went in the back way to the house and entered by a glass door, and into the kitchen ... Mr Whelan and Mrs Whelan was [sic] there, in the kitchen and after a few minutes he and I went into the parlour ... We had two drinks each. One of the daughters went for the drinks. I cannot say whether it was Cissie or Norah [sic]. No one came into the room while I was there. I remained there roughly about half an hour, and I then left by the same way, passed through the kitchen and out by the same door. When passing through the kitchen I saw Jack Galvin of Fox's Castle and Edmond Dunphy sitting at the fire. I spoke to them and they answered me. I remained talking to them for a few minutes ... I did not see Larry Griffin at all that day. There was no one else in Whelan's while I was there as far as I know, but there could be people in the bar or other parts of the house and I would not see them. After returning home I sat at the fire with my sisters for the rest of the night. Nobody spoke to me with regard to keeping my mouth shut. I did not see Thomas Cashin that day.

Chief Superintendent O'Mara did not believe Hannigan's statement, but there was nothing more to be got from him.

During all this time the search of the mineshaft at Ballina-sisla was continuing, without result. However, the search for the body now began to be expanded to other areas. The gardaí used a boat to drag the water in an old slate quarry at a place called Carroll's Cross near Kilmacthomas on the main road between Waterford and Dungarvan. A farmer had reported seeing what resembled a human body floating in a quarry hole, but the guards eventually came to the conclusion that what he had seen was just a sheep's carcass.

On Monday 6 February Larry Griffin's wife, Mary, received a strange letter from the publican Patrick Whelan, now being held with the other suspects in Ballybricken prison.

Dear Mrs Griffin,

So far no trace of poor Larry … Must have Mexican blood to have done this. That day I called down to see you it's little I thought I would be here today. I told you that day when the Guards would finish we would have a try, but I did not get a chance of it. Aren't they desperate men to think people would do such a thing? What harm, but our best friend, Larry – after 18 long years. It took a long time to think it out. I am getting a party to try the bog on Saturday. If you could ask Jack [Mrs Griffin's son] to see Roach [a friend of the Griffin family] and some other hardy chap to give a hand. They will meet the others outside, and you will surely find poor Larry on Sunday. As I told you that day, these fellows did not try the bog at all – only walked over it. I have written to a great friend of mine in Carrick, who will be there to direct; and God knows, the Guards would never find him at the rate they are going. Tell the little girl to write and let me know how you are getting on, as it must have been a terrible ordeal on you.

Yours faithfully,

P. Whelan

The notion that the guards had only 'walked over' the Glen Bog and had not searched it properly is at odds with the accounts of several observers. As the *Waterford Weekly Star* for example reported:

> In the first stages of the search for Griffin's body hardly any portion of this bog was overlooked. The search there was of the most thorough and lasting character both by gardaí and civilians, yet not a sign could be discovered to indicate the presence of the body.

Indeed the postman's son Jack participated with the gardaí in the search of the bog, and would surely have protested if it had not been a thorough job.

Whelan's protestations of his innocence and his suggestion that Mrs Griffin should cooperate with him in organising a search independent of the gardaí did not convince Mrs Griffin. As soon as she received the letter she took it to the gardaí. In fact, Mrs Griffin expressed a strong hope that it would solve the mystery of the disappearance of her husband. It is clear, therefore, that she saw Patrick Whelan as somebody who knew what had happened to Larry, and the desperate woman was hoping that the letter was in some way a genuine indication of the location of her husband's body. If Larry's body was in the bog, she believed it must have been put there by third parties. She told the *Waterford Weekly Star* that he:

had been seventeen years delivering mail on this route and there was not a stop of the way that would be unknown to him. It was altogether unlikely that he would have wandered into the bog, which he knew so intimately.

However, Chief Superintendent O'Mara told the *Irish Independent* that the gardaí 'were perfectly satisfied from the thorough search they had made previously, that Griffin's body was not in the bog'. He told the newspaper that there was no intention of searching the bog again.

As well as losing their husband and father, Mary Griffin and her family had also lost their only source of income: Larry's post-office wages. There was neither a state pension nor a post-office pension for widows in 1929. A group of prominent citizens, moved by the family's plight, set up a fund to assist them and appealed through the press to the public for contributions. The trustees of the fund included the editors of all the local newspapers and the chairman of Waterford County Council. The priests of Kilmacthomas parish were also on the committee, but the priests of Stradbally parish were not.

On 6 February, the day before the commencement of the hearing of the state's preliminary case against the accused, the following extraordinary article appeared in a Waterford-based newspaper, the *Evening News*:

Where a capital charge is made, it is necessary for the Press to print nothing which might in any way interfere with the action of the authorities. At the time that the charge of murder against certain people in Stradbally was made, the story which was current in the district was related to us, but we did not think it right to publish it. However we observe that other newspapers are printing this story, which is briefly, that on Christmas night the family in Mr Whelan's house were engaged with some friends in their best room. Griffin had called at Mr Whelan's house earlier in the day and had been greeted there by a number of his friends. As he was about to leave the premises he pulled his handkerchief out of his trousers pocket and with the handkerchief came three half-crowns which fell on the floor to the bar. As he was riding away on his bicycle a man informed him of the loss of the half-crowns. Griffin then returned to the public house and accosting the first man present mentioned his lost coins and charged him with picking them up.

Griffin's manner was none too mild, especially when he was met with a denial. At once aroused, he caught the man by the lapels of the coat, and they both reached the kitchen … They were both then in the kitchen and the reply to the accusation of 'Liar' was a blow to Griffin's jaw. The blow knocked him down and in the fall he came heavily on the side of his head against the top edge of the American stove, sustaining a long gaping wound on the temple. The man then left. There was but one witness of the miserable incident, a woman seated in the kitchen. She raised the alarm, and some of those upstairs came down, while someone came in from the bar. Griffin appeared to be dead. As to the disposal of the body, the story that the Guards are acting on is that it was wrapped in a blanket with a 56lb weight and taken in a motor to Ballinasisla shaft, whose bottom is covered with many feet of mud.

A similar article appeared in the *Cork Examiner* on the same date. While some of the details of the story differ from Jim Fitzgerald's statement, the essential elements are the same. It is clear therefore that the story of Larry Griffin's death in Whelan's pub, and of the disposal of his body, was widely believed in Stradbally even before Fitzgerald gave his statement to the gardaí. However, the publication of this article by the *Evening News* and the *Cork Examiner* at this point in the legal proceedings was irresponsible and reckless. No one had been convicted of any crime yet and it would be hard to deny that a reasonable reading of the article was that the Whelan family had been involved in covering up the postman's death. The *Evening News* and the *Cork Examiner* paid dearly at a later stage for this error of judgement.

Chapter 12

Despite the harsh windy weather, a crowd of spectators had gathered in front of Waterford courthouse at 10.45 a.m. on Friday 7 February 1930 hoping to see the accused persons in the missing postman case. The imposing classical style of the courthouse, set in its own grounds, made it one of the most prominent buildings in Waterford city. Its grandeur, however, belied a tragic history – it had been built by the hungry poor of Waterford between 1846 and 1849 as a famine-relief project. When the two garda motor cars carrying the prisoners arrived, the spectators surged round trying to catch a glimpse of them but the gardaí closed in around them and hurried them into the building. The two guards among the defendants wore civilian clothes.

Earlier that morning the prosecuting barrister Mr Finlay and the Waterford state solicitor Mr E. A. Ryan had interviewed their star witness, Jim Fitzgerald, in Chief Superintendent O'Mara's office at Lady Lane barracks. According to O'Mara's account, not only did Fitzgerald repeat all he had said in his statement, but he added the sensational detail that Griffin was still breathing when he was wrapped up in the blanket: 'He actually demonstrated for Mr Finlay the way he was breathing at that time.' If true, this would clearly have made it a case of cold-blooded murder, rather than just a cover-up of a tragic accident. So convinced were Mr Finlay and Mr Ryan of Fitzgerald's credibility that they decided to put him on the stand as their very first witness.

Among the crowd inside the courtroom were many members of the local, national and overseas press, including correspondents from the *Daily Express* and the *Daily Mirror*. At 10.46 a.m. Mr F. J. McCabe, district justice, took his seat on the bench, and dealt with some minor cases first. Mr McCabe, noticing the excited crowd and aware of the intense public interest in what was shortly to take place, decided to stamp his authority on proceedings early on. He announced that if there was any noise that would interfere with the business of the court he would clear the court without further warning.

At 11.24 a.m. the missing postman case was called. The accused then entered the dock in the order in which they had been charged. Mrs Whelan and Nora Whelan were accommodated with seats in the front row. James Whelan and Thomas Cashin were seated beside them. Captain William Redmond appeared for the two garda defendants, Ned Dullea and William Murphy. As well as being a practising barrister, Redmond was a Teachta Dála (TD) for Waterford and the leader of the Irish National League Party in the Dáil. His late father John Redmond had been the leader of the old Irish Parliamentary Party in pre-independence days. Mr H. D. Keane appeared for Ned Morrissey, and Mr M. J. Connolly appeared for the rest of the defendants.

When the prisoners had been charged, Mr Finlay opened the case for the prosecution. This was not yet a full murder trial. It was, rather, a preliminary hearing where the prosecutor only had to show that he had sufficient evidence to justify returning the defendants for a full jury trial, and Finlay was convinced that this was merely a formality. His manner of address was formal and dispassionate, but what he had to say was all the more dramatic for that. All of the accused listened to him intently, anxious to find out exactly what case the state was going to make against them:

> The issue before the court today relates to the disappearance of a rural postman named Laurence Griffin, who made certain postal deliveries in the village of Stradbally on Christmas Day last, and has never since been seen. The fact that his body or himself have not been seen since that date has imparted rather an air of mystery into this case, but I hope to be in a position to put facts before the court today that will unravel the mystery. The facts are anything but mysterious – they are simple and I think when the court hears them, you will agree that they speak for themselves.
>
> It appears that between 7 and 8 o'clock on Christmas Day, Laurence Griffin entered the licensed premises of the defendant

Patrick Whelan in Stradbally after the departure from Stradbally that evening of Sergeant Cullinane and one of the Guards. It appears that some of the other inhabitants also took the opportunity of repairing to Whelan's licensed premises.

At about 9 o'clock that night there were a number of the local people in Whelan's house. With them was Griffin.

A number of them were in the bar, which is situated at the front of the house. Among them were the defendants Cashin, Morrissey, Cunningham and Patrick Whelan. At any rate they were certainly there up to a certain stage. Laurence Griffin was also in the bar. Morrissey, Cashin and the deceased as it were, formed one group in the bar.

Griffin was considerably under the influence of drink and while in the bar he apparently dropped some money from his pocket. This was picked up by Morrissey. Griffin objected to Morrissey picking up the money, and words followed between them. Apparently Cashin joined in the dispute. Not many words passed and the next thing that happened was that Cashin struck Griffin a blow and at the same time Morrissey gave him a push. As a result Griffin fell forward on his face and hands and as he did so he came into contact with the stove and from that moment, apparently, he never stirred. Morrissey went forward to pick him up, and turned him over, and one or two others came forward and spoke to him. The prisoner Whelan said: 'You have killed a man in my house'.

A conversation took place and Cashin and Morrissey

133

suggested getting rid of Griffin. Nobody thought to get a priest or a doctor for the unfortunate man who lay there on the floor. Nobody thought of even whispering a prayer in his ear. Apparently the thought uppermost in everybody's mind was: 'We will get rid of Griffin and hide up this thing'. Cashin said: 'I'll go and get my car'. Mrs Whelan came downstairs with a blanket in which to wrap the body of poor Griffin. Then, I suggest that Griffin, not dead, still breathing, was wrapped in this blanket and carried out, not a dead man, and perhaps not beyond medical aid. All that was seen was a mark in the centre of his forehead. The whole discussion was: 'Where shall we put him?' Cashin and Morrissey suggested Kilmacthomas, probably to drop Griffin over the bridge. In any event, Griffin was wrapped up in the blanket, carried by Whelan, Cashin, Morrissey and Cummins via the back of the house, thrown into the waiting motor car, and driven off by Cashin and Morrissey. That was the last ever seen of Laurence Griffin.

I will try to prove that Griffin was not dead when he was removed. He was then a live man, and I suggest that the various acts alleged against the accused persons bring home to them the crime of murder in the first degree.

Civic Guards Murphy and Dullea were on Whelan's premises that evening. It is probable that they were not in the bar when Griffin was struck the blow, but they entered the bar before the body was removed, and they also took steps to see that Griffin's body was taken away. In fact, out of their minds came the suggestions: 'We will take Griffin's bicycle and take it out on the

Chapel Road', apparently to make it appear that Griffin fell from his bicycle and was killed in that way.

According to a newspaper report, great surprise showed on all faces when Mr Finlay then confidently called Jim Fitzgerald to the stand. There was a rustle in the court as everyone craned their necks to get a look at the man 'whose mysterious absence from home had proved only a whit less sensational than Griffin's' as the *Irish Independent* put it. It must have seemed to Finlay that he was about to score a great success in this high-profile case. But, as Fitzgerald climbed down from his seat among the spectators and walked to the witness box, it was noted that he looked exceedingly ill at ease. 'He slumped into the chair, and sat there hunched up, stolid, impassive, looking as if he found all this publicity unpleasant.' Fitzgerald began his evidence, led by questions from Finlay which were asked in a soft soothing tone of voice. Having told the court where he lived and that Tommy Corbett and his wife were lodgers in his house, he started to recount his movements on Christmas Day:

On Christmas day last I went to second mass at eleven o'clock and returned to Knockhouse after. I stayed at home for dinner and tea and after tea about six o'clock I went to Stradbally with Thomas Corbett. We went first to Whelan's corner and we had with us Jim Murphy and Patrick Cunningham.

So far so good. Everything was going according to Finlay's plan. But then there was a moment of confusion as Fitzgerald departed from the script:

> We stayed outside the licensed premises of Patrick Whelan. We got the drink handed out, a bottle of stout each. From there we went over to Riley's [sic] public house and had a bottle of stout each and went inside for it.

But what about going around to the back of Whelan's? What about going in by the kitchen door? What about seeing all the defendants and the missing postman there? One can only imagine the alarm and confusion among the prosecution and the investigating guards in the court, as Fitzgerald proceeded to totally contradict his own witness statement. Finlay's soft soothing tone now became sharp and incisive, as he gazed intently at Fitzgerald and tried to steer him back towards the content of his original witness statement, but Fitzgerald continued on his new and inconvenient course:

> Then we went into the local club and remained there for about an hour. There were people there playing cards. From the Club we, the four of us … went home and on the way we stood at Whelan's corner for a while and then separated and went home.

Sensing the panic in the prosecution ranks, Mr M. J. Connolly rose to his feet to object to Finlay's efforts to get Fitzgerald to give the answers he was looking for. Connolly asked that the witness should be allowed to give his own evidence in his own way, without Finlay's leading questions. The judge agreed. Mr Finlay then resumed his examination, but Fitzgerald showed an obvious reluctance to answer his questions. The prosecuting counsel then appealed to the judge for permission to treat Fitzgerald as a hostile witness. The judge admitted that Fitzgerald appeared to be a very reluctant witness but this led to sharp exchanges with the defence counsel:

Mr Finlay: The witness is attempting to go back on a statement he has already made.

Mr Connolly: This is the first time in the past fortnight that the witness has been at liberty.

Justice McCabe: Mr Connolly, you may make submissions as to whether the witness is hostile or not, but you may not make allegations of that kind.

Mr Connolly: I propose to prove any statement I make. The witness has been in a civic guard barrack in Waterford for the past eight or nine days. He has now been brought into open court to give evidence. But because of something that apparently must have been going on in the barracks, it is now discovered that he is a hostile witness. I submit that he is a fair witness.

Justice McCabe: You first stated that he was not at liberty. All

137

I have to say is that I have no hesitation in holding him as a hostile witness on account of his demeanour.

Mr Finlay then commenced his cross-examination of a very reluctant and uncooperative Fitzgerald:

Finlay: Do you see the name James Fitzgerald signed to written [*sic*] statement which I now hand you?

Fitzgerald: Yes.

Finlay: Is that your signature?

Fitzgerald: Yes.

Finlay: Is that a statement you made to Chief Superintendent O'Mara on 23 January last?

Fitzgerald: Yes, but I may have told some lies about it.

Mr Finlay then read a long portion of Fitzgerald's original statement to the court, describing Fitzgerald's movements on Christmas night up until the point he allegedly entered Whelan's by the back kitchen door and saw Mrs Whelan and Mary Jack Hannigan there.

Finlay: Did you go into Whelan's kitchen and see there Miss Whelan and Mary Jack Hannigan on the evening referred to in the statement?

Fitzgerald: No it was false.

Justice McCabe: Is Mary Jack Hannigan a man or a woman?

The two women prisoners, Mrs Whelan and Nora Whelan, laughed aloud when the judge asked this question.

Fitzgerald: A woman.

There was a burst of laughter in the court, in which all the prisoners joined – they were obviously quite happy at the turn events had taken.

Mr Finlay then read a further portion of Fitzgerald's statement in which he had described seeing Nora and Cissie Whelan in the sitting-room at the piano. According to the statement Garda Dullea was singing and Mr Whelan was in the bar, and not sober. When the reference to Mr Whelan was read Mrs Whelan and Nora Whelan again laughed aloud. The statement went on to describe the death of Griffin and the suggestions for disposing of his body. Then Mr Finlay resumed his cross-examination:

Finlay: Do you say that is false?
Fitzgerald: I do.
Finlay: What part of it is false?

Fitzgerald made no reply and Mr Finlay repeated the question three times.

Fitzgerald: I could not swear what is lies.

Finlay: What part is false?

Fitzgerald: I swear that I did not see the man at all.

When the question was repeated Fitzgerald said: 'I have no more to say.'

When questioned further he said that he could not say what part of the statement was false, and he said that Larry Griffin was not in Whelan's at all on Christmas night.

Finlay: What part of your statement is true, then?

Fitzgerald: That he was not there at all.

Finlay: Do you know that you never said that in your statement?

Justice McCabe: Why did you make these statements to the chief superintendent if they were not true?

Fitzgerald: There were a lot of things forced out of me.

Finlay: So they were in you, and it was only a matter of getting them out of you?

Fitzgerald: Yes.

Finlay: Do you suggest that you made up this statement?

Fitzgerald: A lot of it.

Finlay: What parts?

Fitzgerald: About Griffin.

Finlay: Were all these other people you mentioned in Whelan's house on that evening?

Fitzgerald: I would not say.

Finlay: Was Morrissey there?

Fitzgerald: He may be there unknown to me.

Finlay: Was Cashin in there?

Fitzgerald: He may be there unknown to me.

Finlay: Was Patrick Whelan in the house?

Fitzgerald: It seems he was.

Finlay: Was Guard Dullea in the house?

Fitzgerald: I wouldn't swear that.

Finlay: Was Guard Murphy in the house?

Fitzgerald: I wouldn't swear that.

Finlay: Did you hear the piano playing?

Fitzgerald: I don't know.

Finlay: Are you deaf? (much laughter from dock)

Fitzgerald: No.

Finlay: Did you hear a piano playing in the sitting-room?

Fitzgerald: I did not.

Finlay: Did you hear any songs being sung?

Fitzgerald: I did not.

Finlay: Did you see Master Cashin any time that evening?

Fitzgerald: I saw him in the street about six or seven o'clock, after going to Whelan's corner.

Finlay: Did you see Morrissey?

Fitzgerald: No.

Finlay: Did you get a drink either inside or outside Whelan's?

Fitzgerald: I got a drink outside but didn't go inside.

Finlay: Why did you make up the story?

There was a pause as Fitzgerald remained silent. Then Finlay pressed him again and Fitzgerald answered:

> **Fitzgerald:** I couldn't help it; there was a lot of it forced out of me.
>
> **Finlay:** Did you mention the names of Cashin, Morrissey, Paddy Whelan and Mrs Whelan and the Cummins?
>
> **Fitzgerald:** Yes.
>
> **Finlay:** What did you say about Cashin?
>
> **Fitzgerald:** I could not swear I said anything.
>
> **Finlay:** If you mentioned people's names, was it not in connection with the disappearance of Laurence Griffin?
>
> **Fitzgerald:** I suppose it was.

As Finlay finished his cross-examination he must have been extremely frustrated with the turn that events had taken. Mr Connolly, representing seven of the defendants, then proceeded to question Fitzgerald:

> **Connolly:** Where have you been for the last ten days?
>
> **Fitzgerald:** Above in Lady Lane barracks.
>
> **Connolly:** When were you brought there?
>
> **Fitzgerald:** A fortnight tomorrow.
>
> **Connolly:** Had you any desire to stay there?
>
> **Fitzgerald:** They kept me there. I'd be anxious to go home.
>
> **Connolly:** They kept you there?

Fitzgerald: I'd rather stay there than at home.

Justice McCabe: And why did you prefer to remain in the barracks instead of going home. Can you answer that?

Fitzgerald: I could not. Well, they kept me there.

Fitzgerald was contradicting himself and making little sense. Justice McCabe intervened to ask him again why he preferred to remain in the barracks:

Fitzgerald: I have no objection to going home now.

The exasperated judge continued to question him on these lines, when Mr Connolly interrupted and said that the witness had already answered the question.

Justice McCabe: I have not received an answer, only evasions, and I intend to question him until I do.

Connolly: Until you get a certain answer.

Justice McCabe: That remark does you no credit, and I am taking no notice of it, Mr Connolly.

The judge questioned Fitzgerald again but failed to get any clear answer out of him, and then read his witness statement over to him again, but he still got nowhere with the witness. Fitzgerald was finally excused and, despite what he had just said, he allowed himself to be escorted back to Lady Lane barracks by the gardaí. Mr Finlay for the prosecution said that he had no further evidence to offer that day and asked for a week's remand. Captain Redmond applied for bail for Guards Dullea and Murphy, against whom, he submitted, no evidence whatever had been adduced. In response to Redmond's application the judge replied: 'Captain Redmond, your clients are charged with murder. If counsel for the attorney-general says that he will be able to connect them with this charge I cannot grant bail.' Mr Connolly asked if Mr Finlay would be in a position at a later stage to give some evidence to back up the prosecution case. 'Yes,' answered Finlay, even though he knew that he had no other significant evidence to offer. Fitzgerald's testimony was to have been the main thrust of his case. Mr Connolly continued:

> My clients are under arrest and they are anxious to meet at the earliest moment all the evidence that can possibly be brought connecting them in any way with the disappearance of poor Griffin. My clients are very respectable and favourably known persons, and I think that your worship should intimate that within a fixed period evidence should be produced to justify my clients being kept in custody. There is the fact that if Griffin is dead his body had not been found and there is no proof of his killing before the court.

Mr Keane spoke in similar terms on behalf of Morrissey. The judge remanded all the prisoners in custody for a week. They were then removed from the court. There was a large crowd of people gathered again outside the courthouse to see them driven away. Two cars were drawn up outside the front of the building, but they were decoys, for the prisoners were hurried out the back entrance into two cars which were waiting there with their blinds drawn. The Whelans entered one car, the other defendants entered the second, and they were driven back to Ballybricken prison. The *Waterford Weekly Star* reported that 'large numbers again gathered outside the jail, and as the prisoners were brought into the jail, their friends from Stradbally district cheered them lustily'.

Reviewing the proceedings, the *Irish Independent's* reporter wrote: 'Sensations were expected at Waterford district Court today but I doubt if anyone expected them to be quite as sensational as they turned out to be.'

Chapter 13

General O'Duffy was furious when he heard about the fiasco in Waterford district court, and he directed that Chief Superintendent O'Mara should come to garda HQ that very evening. When O'Mara reached Dublin, O'Duffy's temper had not calmed down, and it seems that they had a very tempestuous meeting, in which, according to O'Mara's account, O'Duffy suggested that Fitzgerald's original statement had been beaten out of him and threatened the superintendent with dismissal. After some time, according to O'Mara, the commissioner said that he knew quite well, from the information he had received while in Waterford, that Griffin's body wasn't in the mineshaft but was buried in some freshly made grave in one of the cemeteries in the vicinity of Stradbally – that it was either in a coffin under the one which had been last interred or was perhaps under the corpse in a coffin:

> He turned to me then and said 'you go back to Waterford tomorrow and have all the freshly made graves opened and examined'. I said, quite innocently, that we'd require exhumation orders for that. He

then said: 'Are you refusing to obey the commissioner's orders?
Do you want to go to Donegal?' He became furious and raged
for some time … I persisted, in a respectful way, and said that I
didn't mind to where I might be sent and that I had never refused
to obey the order of a superior but that I wished to point out the
sacred regard everybody had for the bones of dead relatives and the
indignation which unauthorised and indiscriminate interference
with graves would create amongst the clergy and laity. I said that
I had even heard of instances in which the opening by mistake, of
another's grave to inter a corpse had led to loss of life and added
that if anybody disturbed the bones of a near relative of mine, I
would stop at nothing to effect a speedy and heavy punishment.
He abused me in a very biting and personal way, without one
retort, until he got tired and then he retired.

While O'Mara's account of this encounter may be rather par-
tial, it is clear that the turn the investigation had taken, for the
gardaí, was leading to recriminations within the force – hence
O'Mara's desire to record his own version of events for posterity.
In any case, O'Mara did get his official exhumation orders and
returned to County Waterford to put them into effect.

Meanwhile, Jim Fitzgerald finally returned to his house in
Stradbally the day after his dramatic court appearance, having
spent a fortnight in Lady Lane barracks. He was driven back to
the village from Waterford in a garda car. The *Irish Independent*
wrote:

Little notice was taken of Fitzgerald's return in the village, although the news of it must have spread rapidly, for if they talk little to outsiders, the villagers have a marvellous facility for keeping themselves au fait with everything that transpires.

On Sunday morning Fitzgerald attended second mass in Stradbally. He went alone and returned home alone, although a few people did catch his glance and nod to him in greeting. The *Irish Independent* reporter called up to his house after mass and asked him about his situation:

He pondered deeply before he replied. 'It's a bothersome case', was his verdict. 'I hope I'm out of it but I may be called to give evidence again.' He told me that on Thursday, 23 January, the guards sent for him and brought him to Stradbally barracks at about 9 p.m. There he was interviewed by Chief Superintendent O'Mara and a detective in a room in which there were about eight members of the gardaí. On Saturday night they brought him to his house to pack some clothes, and then he went with them to Lady's Lane barracks. The guards, he said, were very friendly. He was very comfortable, was well fed, and had a bed as good as a man could ask for. The guards did not say much to him about his repudiation of his statement. He did not get any expenses as a witness; nor did he ask for them.

The idea that the gardaí did not say much to Fitzgerald about his repudiation of his original statement is hard to believe, and makes one wonder whether his glowing account of his treatment by them while in the barracks had more to do with a fear of the gardaí than with the reality of how they had dealt with him. However, his account of being brought in for questioning by the gardaí clearly contradicts Chief Superintendent O'Mara's claim that Fitzgerald had come into the station of his own accord. The reference to eight other gardaí being present during the questioning also paints a different picture from that which O'Mara had drawn. Being faced with such a large number of gardaí during such a stressful interrogation would have been very intimidating for a man like Jim Fitzgerald, regardless of what other kinds of pressure may have been brought to bear upon him.

Apart from mass time, the streets of Stradbally were deserted that Sunday, other than the few gardaí who were on duty. Over in Kilmacthomas, Larry Griffin's wife Mary was seen to be in a very depressed state, for she had come to accept that her husband was dead.

By now, Chief Superintendent O'Mara had ascertained the location of the various graveyards within striking distance of Stradbally and the positions of the graves in which corpses had been recently interred. In the dead of night, 'which was the only time which we could shake off the press men who had at least five cars scouting after the police cars', the graveyards were visited by a specially selected party of gardaí led by O'Mara.

They opened the graves, extracted the coffins, opened the coffins, and lifted out the corpses to check underneath them. 'Nobody who hasn't had the experience of the sickening smell from the encased decomposing corpse and the clammy feel of the fishy-like flesh can appreciate the ordeal those men faced night after night for over a fortnight until their task was done,' wrote O'Mara. Over twenty-four graves in six graveyards were checked unknown to the press and public.

However, the public were well aware of the continuing search at the Ballinasisla mineshaft. The area was visited by thousands of people from all parts of County Waterford and even further afield. Local bus operators cashed in on the excitement by running regular trips from Waterford city and other places. Motor cars and horse-drawn cars were also in high demand. As well as inspecting the Ballinasisla site, many of the visitors to the district wandered through the fields, where there was a network of mineshafts, and they tested their depth by flinging large stones into them and listening to the splash in the water far below.

This huge public interest in the case only added to the pressure on An Garda Síochána. The prosecution had bluffed in court that they still had a strong case against the accused and the judge had given them the benefit of the doubt – hence the increasingly frantic efforts to find a body. In an unprecedented expenditure of public funds in the search for a body, the gardaí now commissioned the construction of a great wooden frame over the mineshaft at Ballinasisla, and the putting in place of a much more powerful and effective dredging apparatus. The latter consisted of a large clamp grab, which could be lowered to the bottom of the shaft by cables. The grab, which had teeth, opened into two sections when being lowered, and as it reached the mud at the bottom it would close on any object that might be there, after which it would be hauled back to the surface. It took a full day to construct the grab and another to get it working properly. In the days leading up to the second court appearance the grab was raised and lowered repeatedly, with no result. It was becoming increasingly apparent that if the body was in the mineshaft, it was useless to continue trying to fish it up in this way. The gardaí even consulted engineers about the possibility of pumping out the mineshaft, an operation that, even if possible, would have cost £20,000 to £25,000 – an enormous sum of money in 1930. Naturally enough, they were reluctant to undertake this expenditure unless they could come up with some tangible proof that the body was in the mine, and so they continued to lower the grab in the hope of finding at least a portion of the postman's clothing, his bag or some such article.

It was a full and excited courtroom once more at Waterford for the second appearance of the accused persons, on Friday 14 February. This time the prisoners had been brought to the court an hour early and kept in cells below the dock, to avoid the expected crowds of supporters. Several of the newspapers commented on the large number of 'ladies' who were present in the public gallery. It was also noted that there were several clergymen in attendance. Mr F. J. McCabe, the district justice, once more warned that, if there was any noise from the spectators, he would clear the court without warning. He also stated that earlier in the morning a photographer from an English newspaper had called on him privately and had asked him if he might be allowed to take a photo in court. The justice had promptly told him that he would not permit such a thing for a moment, and he now repeated that refusal in public for the benefit of any other photographers who might be present.

When the accused were brought forward it was observed that their faces were less cheerful than during their previous court appearance. Perhaps their legal counsel had advised them not to be seen to be laughing, as they had at the earlier hearing. Cissie Whelan was in the public gallery, and it was reported that 'she held a brave front, but when her relatives appeared in the dock she was observed to wipe a few tears from her eyes'. Her mother and her sister Nora gave her reassuring smiles.

The first witnesses to be called by Mr Finlay for the state were two of the three Kilmacthomas men who had come to Stradbally on St Stephen's Day looking for Larry Griffin. They repeated their evidence that Patrick Whelan had told them that Larry had been in the pub the night before, that he had been drunk, and that Whelan had tried unsuccessfully to persuade him to stay the night. This evidence contradicted the Whelans' claims that Larry had not been in the public house at all on

Christmas Day. Next up was John Power, the young man who had first said that he saw Garda Dullea with Larry Griffin on Christmas Day. He now gave evidence that he saw the two men going towards Whelan's back gate and that it looked to him as if they had gone into the public house.

Doctor John McGrath, lecturer on medical jurisprudence at UCD and pathologist to the Coombe and Mercer's Hospitals gave evidence next. Of the thirty items of clothing removed from Thomas Cashin's house only one item, a pair of brown trousers, showed a possibly positive result for human blood. There was a narrow bloodstain about 1.8 inches long on the outer side of the left trouser leg. However, due to potential contamination Dr McGrath could not state definitely that it was human blood. Most of the items taken from Thomas Cashin's car tested negative for human blood. One item described as a 'block tin plate taken from the side of the doorway of [the] … motor car' had two small bloodstains. The samples obtained from the stains was so small, however, that the tests for human blood could not be carried out. Of the eight items of clothing taken from Ned Morrissey's house only one item gave a positive result for blood. A pair of dark grey trousers had a stain on the back right trouser leg and another on the outer side of the right trouser leg which gave positive results for blood. Again, however, it was not possible to carry out the tests for human blood because of contamination by dirt. The stove, the stool, the floorboards and other items of furniture taken from Whelan's pub all tested negative for blood. The piece of flannelette, the piece of blanket cloth and lady's stocking found among Nora and Cissie's belongings all tested positive for human blood. However, the pathologist acknowledged that these stains could have been caused if the items had been used for sanitary purposes. A shirt taken from Patrick Whelan's house had six small stains on the upper portion of the front which tested positive for blood, but the stains were too small to perform the tests for human blood. In short, Dr McGrath's evidence was of little use to the prosecution. The tests available to forensic scientists in 1930 were far less advanced than modern methods. The only items which the pathologist could be sure had human bloodstains on them were almost certainly sanitary cloths belonging to the young women in the Whelan household.

It was clear that the prosecution case was foundering. Representing some of the accused, Mr M. J. Connolly reminded the justice that, when the prosecution had opened their case the week before, they had made various allegations including one that the unfortunate postman had been struck by one of the accused persons and taken away by another. Mr Connolly said that he had anticipated that the state would have produced some evidence to support those allegations but that this had not happened:

> These people declare that they are innocent, and they had nothing whatever to do with the disappearance of this postman. They

are prepared to meet this charge anywhere, and to seek the first opportunity to meet it, and they don't want to shirk anything. Unless Mr Finlay is in a position to give further evidence than he has given you now, the matter is entirely at your own discretion, but I would like to protest strongly against keeping them in custody.

Mr Finlay for the prosecution responded angrily, accusing Mr Connolly of insinuating that he had exceeded his professional duty. He argued that the original statement of Jim Fitzgerald which had been produced in court justified every word of his opening statement. He alleged that Mr Connolly 'and his friends' were not perturbed when the statement was being read, 'because apparently they knew what I did not know – that when Fitzgerald went into the witness chair he was going to deny his own statement'. At this point Justice McCabe intervened to prevent further heated exchanges between the prosecution and defence. He agreed to give the prosecution more time to make its case and remanded the accused in custody for another week. According to Chief Superintendent O'Mara's account, the prosecuting counsel, Mr Finlay:

impressed on us that evening the necessity of keeping in touch with Fitzgerald because he said if Fitzgerald came forward then and gave evidence of his original statement the prosecution would be, to use his own expression, sailing before the wind.

The bulk of garda resources, however, was directed towards a massive effort to locate the body of Larry Griffin. A new theory which was pursued was that the body of the postman was buried in the sands or shingle at Stradbally Cove. Twenty members of the force equipped with heavy picks and shovels were detailed to dig up every square inch of the foreshore to a depth of four feet. These digging operations were hampered as the work could only be carried out between tides. It took several days to dig up the entire cove but nothing was found.

It was also reported that local farmers and labourers took it upon themselves to organise yet another search of the Glen Bog, in the belief, encouraged by Patrick Whelan, that the job had not been done properly in two previous searches – one by the people of Stradbally themselves, and one by An Garda Síochána. The *Irish Independent* reporter wrote that he 'never understood why this belief was held so tenaciously by the local people'. He wrote that he had discussed the previous two searches with those who took part in them and that 'it is reasonably certain that the body of any man who strayed into the bog accidentally would have been found'. However, the dedication of the searchers was not in doubt. In bitterly cold weather they searched the bog thoroughly, wading knee deep and barefoot in icy water, precariously perched on improvised duckboards which sank inches into the slime and weeds at every step. On the second day of the search they burned the grass, weeds and bushes from the surface to simplify their task:

From time to time a choking, coughing figure, with tears streaming from the red-rimmed eyes in his smoke-grimed face, would emerge on to the road for a breath of fresh air before plunging once more into those acres of smoke and flame. By late afternoon most of the scrub and grass had been burnt away and the bog was criss-crossed with long, dark, unsightly scars, interspersed with gleaming mirrors of still grey water, but no vestige of human remains was to be seen.

Meanwhile the search at Ballinasisla mineshaft continued and hundreds of sightseers were still coming to watch it. It was reported in *The Irish Times* that 'a long line of motor cars stretched away down to the valley, and hundreds of bicycles were parked on the hill'. The *Irish Independent* estimated that 2,000 people came to visit the site on Sunday 16 February and the special buses from Waterford and Dungarvan were still doing a roaring trade. Garda Inspector Brazil, who was in charge of the operation at the mineshaft, said that his men were now so expert in the work that they could detect even a slight extra weight on the grapple the minute they raised it from the bottom. The *Irish Independent* reporter was highly complimentary about the zeal and enthusiasm of the gardaí working at the mineshaft. He found their cheerfulness as they worked remarkable 'in view of the fact that the search of this shaft enters on its fourth week and that so far nothing but sore hands and extreme personal discomfort has resulted'.

The gardaí had for some time been making enquiries to find a professional diver to explore the Ballinasisla shaft. The diver, Mr F. Morgan of the Liverpool firm Dennison and Sons, arrived at the shaft on 17 February. After some discussions with the gardaí, he was lowered into the shaft on a boson's chair to inspect the mineshaft before carrying out a dive. As he went down he carefully examined the sides of the mineshaft, testing protruding stones and cracks in the hard clay. From time to time he signalled to the gardaí above to stop paying out the cable while he made a more detailed examination of some point. The *Irish Independent's* reporter wrote that it 'was an eerie experience to watch that tiny figure on the swaying chair, slowly sinking until it looked like a minute marionette slowly revolving at the end of the rope'. The first descent lasted well over a quarter of an hour and then the signal to haul up was given. Mr Morgan was very reticent when he reached the top, but he mentioned that the water was quite clear and that when he had been near the surface he could see to a depth of ten or twelve feet. This seemed to be a positive indication, because it had been feared that the water would be too muddy for a diver to see anything, even if he did go beneath the surface. After another descent into the shaft Mr Morgan travelled to Waterford where he made a disappointing report to Chief Superintendent O'Mara – the mineshaft was in too dangerous a condition to risk sending down divers. In an interview with the *Irish Independent* Mr Morgan said that 'the mine shaft was the narrowest he had ever seen. For this reason it would prove a veritable death-trap for men working below should any earth or stones become dislodged from the sides.' Mr Morgan pointed out that, owing to the great depth of the shaft, even a fairly small stone would be travelling with the force of a bullet by the time it neared the surface of the water and, owing to the exceedingly small diameter of the shaft, anything that fell would be almost certain to hit one of the men working on the shaft below. He pointed out that the mineshaft had not been worked for years and consequently its sides were insecure, and that a swaying cable rubbing against the side might precipitate a number of stones or even a big section from the wall of the shaft into the depths below. Under the circumstances, he considered it far too hazardous to attempt to dive in the shaft.

It was also becoming clear that pumping out the mine was not a feasible project. A Waterford-based engineer told *The Irish Times* that:

> to pump out would be a colossal task, costing a huge sum if it were to be done properly. I think there is not a pumping appa-ratus in Ireland that would be able to cope with the work, so that equipment must be brought from England, as well as men to work it. Even then complete failure may be met.

Chief Superintendent O'Mara still believed that the Ballina-sisla mineshaft was the most likely location for the body, but the diver's negative report was a big setback with the next court date fast approaching. The gardaí continued the dredging operation, but with diminishing hopes of success.

Larry Griffin during his service
in the British army in India.
(*Reproduced with permission of
Bridie Griffin*)

Larry Griffin with his wife Mary.
(*Reproduced with permission of
Bridie Griffin*)

Larry Griffin and family. *Back row left to right:* Jack, Larry. *Front row left to right:* Alice, Bridie, Mary. *(Reproduced with permission of Bridie Griffin)*

Kilmacthomas post office.

A garda stands over Larry Griffin's bicycle where it was found on the Stradbally to Kilmacthomas road. The camera is looking in the direction of Kilmacthomas. *(Reproduced with permission of the Garda Museum and Archives)*

Uniformed gardaí and detectives at the location where Larry Griffin's bicycle was found. The camera is looking towards Stradbally. *(Reproduced with permission of the Garda Museum and Archives)*

Whelan's corner. *(Reproduced with permission of the Garda Museum and Archives)*

The square in Stradbally. Whelan's pub and the post office are the first two houses in the terrace on the left. Garda Patrick Frawley lived above the post office. The two-storey house to the right of the photograph is McGrath's or 'the hall'. *(Reproduced with permission of the Garda Museum and Archives)*

The square in Stradbally. The three-storey house on the right is the garda barracks. *(Reproduced with permission of the Garda Museum and Archives)*

The square in Stradbally. Thomas Cashin's house is on the far left of the photograph. Whelan's pub and the post office can be seen to the right. *(Reproduced with permission of the Garda Museum and Archives)*

The Chapel Road, Stradbally. On the left a detective stands at Whelan's back gate. In the centre another detective stands at Whelan's corner. On the right a uniformed garda stands near the old ruins. *(Reproduced with permission of the Garda Museum and Archives)*

A photograph which includes Thomas Cashin and Ned Morrissey, taken in 1960. Cashin is on the far left and Morrissey on the far right.

Some of the defendants in the missing
postman case, taken outside Waterford
District Court on 7 February 1930. The photographs were printed in the *Irish Independent* the
following day.

Top: Garda Murphy (left), Garda Dullea (centre)
      and Edmund Morrisey (right)
Above left: Patrick Whelan
Above right: James and Nora Whelan
Right: Thomas F. Cashin

SEARCH FOR MISSING POSTMAN.

Civic Guards are seen above strenuously engaged in grappling operations at the Bonmahon mine-shaft.

Laurence Griffin, the missing Co. Waterford postman, with his bicycle and mail bag. (Exclusive to the "Cork Examiner").

Photographs from the *Cork Examiner* show the gardaí searching the Tankardstown mine-shaft near Bunmahon, and Larry Griffin in his postman's uniform.

The search of the Ballinasisla mineshaft. *(Reproduced with permission of the Garda Museum and Archives)*

A crowd gathers to observe the search of the Ballinasisla mineshaft. *(Reproduced with permission of the Garda Museum and Archives)*

Garda Commissioner General Eoin O'Duffy. *(Reproduced with permission of the Garda Museum and Archives)*

Assistant Commissioner Éamonn Coogan. *(Reproduced with permission of the Garda Museum and Archives)*

Painting of Chief Super-
intendent Harry O'Mara.
*(Reproduced with permission
of the Garda Museum and
Archives)*

Superintendent James Hunt.
*(Reproduced with permission
of Maureen Doherty)*

Garda John Sullivan. *(Reproduced with permission of Pauline Clifford)*

Garda John Sullivan in front of Stradbally barracks with his family. *(Reproduced with permission of Pauline Clifford)*

Garda Peter Twamley (on the left), one of the officers brought in to investigate the missing postman case. *(Reproduced with permission of the Garda Síochána Retired Members Association)*

Ex-Garda William Murphy (back row, far right) with the Bruree camogie team sometime in the 1940s.

Ex-Garda William Murphy (front row, far right) with the Bruree hurling team about 1948.

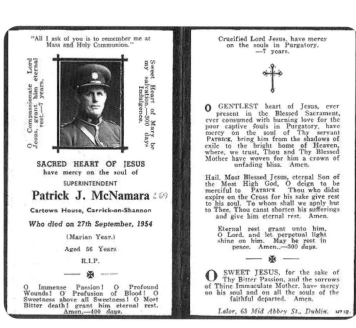

Inspector Patrick McNamara (photograph on memorial card). *(Reproduced with permission of the Garda Museum and Archives)*

Postman Mike Murphy, Larry Griffin's successor, being presented with a clock and gift of money by Norah Whelan, wife of James Whelan, in 1955. *(Reproduced with permission of Seán Murphy)*

Mike Murphy, with James and Norah Whelan, 1955. *(Reproduced with permission of Seán Murphy)*

The stretch of road near Ballyvoile Bridge under which lies Larry Griffin's body according to local folklore. *(Photograph taken by the author)*

Right: Leo Griffin, Bridie Griffin and Willie Griffin (from left to right) outside the family business at Kilmacthomas. *(Photograph taken by the author)*

Below: Stradbally village today. Whelan's pub is on the left. *(Photograph taken by the author)*

Chapter 14

Only a portion of the huge crowd who came to hear the evidence in the sensational missing postman case managed to gain entry to Waterford courthouse for the third hearing, on Friday 21 February. Among the early arrivals on that frosty morning was a contingent of friends and supporters of the accused who had travelled from Stradbally in a specially chartered bus. Cissie Whelan, the only grown-up member of the Whelan family who had not been arrested and charged, had travelled with the Stradbally group. At 11.20 a.m. the case was called and the ten defendants entered the dock. There was a distinct change in their appearances compared with previous court sittings. 'Today all the accused are showing the strain of their last four weeks and of the confinement,' reported the *Irish Independent*.

The most significant evidence was given by Mrs Brigid Frawley, wife of Garda Frawley. She repeated what she had already said in her recent statements, that Garda Dullea and the postman had been together in her house on Christmas Day, that the postman was clearly drunk, and that he, Dullea and her husband had left together, although her husband had returned shortly afterwards. She also told of Dullea later asking her not to say that she had seen him in the company of Larry Griffin on Christmas Day. While the effect of her evidence was to cast suspicion on Garda Dullea, it did nothing to connect Dullea or any of the other defendants directly with Larry Griffin's alleged death. Another witness, Patrick Power, described the comings and goings in the centre of Stradbally on Christmas evening, in particular the fact that Dullea walked around Whelan's corner with the postman who was sick and trying to vomit from the effects of drink. Various gardaí gave evidence relating to maps of the district, to the collection of evidence and to the taking of statements in the case. The prosecuting counsel, Mr Finlay, asked for a further remand of one week. He indicated that this was the last occasion on which he would ask for a remand, and that he would deal with the case finally on the next court day. Counsel for the defendants welcomed this announcement and did not oppose a further remand on that basis. Justice McCabe agreed to the remand request, although he said that 'there may be ten more remands if anything turns up to make me think such remands necessary'.

Indeed at the next court sitting on 1 March Finlay went back on his promise. He produced no new evidence and asked for yet another remand on the basis that the body of Larry Griffin was close to being found. To justify his request he put Garda Superintendent Meehan on the stand:

Meehan: Within the past five days certain information has come into my possession regarding the whereabouts of Griffin's body.

Finlay: Are enquiries being pursued along lines of this information?

Meehan: Yes.

Finlay: Do you consider it is probable that within the next week you will be able to discover the body of Laurence Griffin?

Meehan: I do, sir.

Finlay: Do you pray for a remand for the purpose of making further enquiries?

Meehan: Yes.

Despite very vigorous protests by Captain Redmond and the other defence counsel, Justice McCabe again acquiesced to the prosecution's request and remanded the defendants in custody for a further week. The proceedings then terminated and there was a general rush by relatives and friends of the prisoners to shake hands with them through the bars of the dock. It was reported in the *Munster Express* that all the accused 'appeared quite cheerful', which is not surprising in light of how little evidence had been produced against them.

Among those observing the proceedings was the distressed wife and presumed widow of Larry Griffin, along with her sister and some friends. The constant adjournments, remands and promises of breakthroughs in the case can only have worsened her ordeal. However, the appeal which had been made for financial contributions to help the Griffin family was meeting a very generous response from the public. By now over £100 had been collected, the equivalent of about half a postman's yearly salary. The staff of Sheridan's Motor Garage in Waterford contributed £2 2s and the editor of the *Waterford News* gave £1. About half of the contributions to date had come from residents of Kilmacthomas, but just a few had come from Stradbally. Among the latter was £1 from the Convent of Mercy, £1 from Canon Burkett and £1 from the postmistress Miss Hannigan.

While the public appetite for news about the case of the missing postman remained unabated, the lack of new developments caused difficulties for the press men as they struggled to fill their columns. When the *Irish Independent*'s 'special representative' visited the Ballinasisla mineshaft on the Sunday after the latest court hearing, he discovered that the gardaí there were taking a well-earned day of rest after three weeks of heavy and boring toil. As the garda on duty cheerfully commented: 'We will be the best tug-of-war team in Ireland after this!' There had been occasional articles of possible interest dragged up, such as a portion of a man's vest, but Mrs Griffin had been unable to say if it belonged to her husband and it had been forwarded to Dublin for forensic examination. The constant streams of visitors to the mineshaft that Sunday were loud in their expressions of disappointment at the news, conveyed to them by the garda on duty, that there would be no dragging operations that day, and complained that their Sunday trip had been spoiled.

Stradbally village was also sleepier and more silent that Sunday afternoon than it had been over the previous few weeks, leading the reporter to muse about the character of the local people as a way of filling his column inches:

> There was little activity among the guards there and the villagers pursued the taciturn tenor of their lives. The native of Stradbally seems to have a smaller fund of curiosity than is to be found in any village in Ireland. Yet, as we learned in court a week ago, the comings and goings of even well-known residents are noted and remembered, so that weeks afterwards we can be told the name of every man who passed through the village or crossed the road weeks before. It is the curious quality that gives the village its baffling atmosphere of mystery. It is merely the Stradbally way, self-contained and slightly contemptuous of strangers.

However, the reporter did find one talkative person in Stradbally. This was Mary Jack Hannigan, whose name had featured in some of the court dispatches and who was evidently a bit of a local character:

> Mary is seventy-four, and looks ten or more years younger. A well-preserved woman with a humorous twinkle in her eyes, she has very decided views on modern fashions and manners. 'I was

as strong as any man in my youth,' she said, 'and I worked like a man in the fields and in the mines over at Bunmahon at the place they dressed the copper. I worked in the Tankardstown shaft. The Ballinasisla one was not being worked then and that's over fifty years ago. Those were the days when we worked with our arms. It was the muscles did it then. Now it's all machinery.'

Turning to the question of the modern girl, she seems to think that the hobble skirt was the fashion milestone that marks the fall of woman from the position of serious workers in the world to that of what she contemptuously described as 'useless young flappers'.

Chief Superintendent O'Mara, however, had more serious matters on his mind, as the mood at the garda depot in Dublin was turning decidedly sour against him. O'Mara had sent no significant report to HQ since 18 January, and this resulted in a strongly worded reprimand from Deputy Commissioner Coogan on 24 February. O'Mara promptly dispatched a report in which he wrote that information had been received that the body of Larry Griffin had been in the grounds of Stradbally convent until the night of 21 January (the night the Stradbally gardaí were transferred), and that the body was then removed by car to another location. However, O'Mara's report does not reveal the source of this information. The chief superintendent also introduced in this report a new character to the story of the missing postman – Garda Charles Dullea who was stationed at Ballymacarbery in County Tipperary and who was an older brother of the suspect Garda Edward Dullea. Charles had visited his brother in prison and had attended the hearing of the case in the district court but O'Mara criticised him for not being helpful in 'clearing up the crime':

I am informed that the only source of revenue the two accused gardaí have for their defence is from Garda Charles Dullea and he is, I understand, financing his brother. He has done nothing to assist the prosecution but has been endeavouring to defeat it. Everybody engaged in the investigations and conversant with the characters is agreed that Garda Edward Dullea is the weakest individual of the accused persons and that pressure on him would result in useful information. The most powerful form of pressure which can be brought to bear on him at present would be to indicate that his brother's position is also in jeopardy. This has already been suggested to the brother but he does not appreciate its import and will not until some definite action is taken. It is beyond doubt that Garda Edward Dullea is deeply implicated in the disappearance of Griffin and the subsequent conspiracy of silence. As a result his brother, Charles Dullea, is not a fit member to be in the force and a request for his resignation is justifiable. I believe this would bring the matter home to both and would have the desired result. If I receive authority to do so I will call him to my office and point out the position to him. He should in any event be recalled to the depot immediately.

There is no evidence in the files that Chief Superintendent O'Mara ever received permission to proceed with this plan, and Garda Charles Dullea remained a member of An Garda Síochána for many years to come.

In another sign of the increasing lack of confidence in the chief superintendent's handling of the investigation, while O'Mara was on a visit to HQ, General O'Duffy informed him that he was sending Superintendent James Hunt from Galway to 'assist' him in the investigation. James Hunt was a forty-one-year-old married man, father of seven children and a native of Boyle in County Roscommon. As one of the relatively few veterans of the old RIC in An Garda Síochána he would have had an edge over many in the force in terms of professional policing experience. When Superintendent Hunt arrived he had his own car and was assisted by Detective Garda Brian Hanley. O'Mara was not pleased about their arrival and in his written account he described them as 'free-lances' who 'travelled within and out of the county at will' and alleged that Detective Hanley was 'a villain devoid of principle, character or police ability'. He also wrote that:

> Superintendent Hunt was reporting direct to HQrs from the time he arrived, although I was given to understand by the commissioner and himself that this wasn't the case, and I am sure if his confidential reports are still available, that they will bear this out.

The investigation files, however, reveal that Superintendent Hunt was not sending reports to HQ at this time. In fact O'Mara's own records prove that Hunt was reporting the results of his investigations to O'Mara personally. It is also clear from the files that Hunt did have a particular ability to gain people's trust. Within days of his arrival Mrs Frawley described him in a letter to her husband as 'a man with a lot of common sense':

> He explained to me that even though you were not in Whelan's when this happened you must have noticed strange movements on the part of Murphy and Dullea during the following days and you are not voicing your suspicions. Now it is not too late yet. You have nothing to do up there in the Depot so sit down and go back and think and think hard. If you noticed anything strange in their movements tell it, it may be nothing and it may mean a whole lot … So now Paddy work up your brains and voice your suspicions …

O'Mara's reports to headquarters give a fascinating insight into the various rumours, hints and theories that were cropping up in the continuing investigation. The chief superintendent now reported a rumour that Fr Burke, one of the local priests, had been in Whelan's on Christmas night when Larry Griffin died:

> He [Fr Burke] was always very unfriendly towards Cashin until St Stephen's Day and he was noticed conversing for a considerable

time with him on that day in an evidently friendly attitude. He has
been calling to Cashin's very frequently since and has said mass in
the house during the past week.

Another priest who was attracting the attention of the gardaí
was Fr M. Dowley in the neighbouring parish of Kill. In his
sermon on Sunday 16 February he publicly criticised the state's
case against the accused persons, saying that he did not believe
that any Christians could do such a thing as they had been
accused of and that people should not be talking about it or
spreading rumours about which they knew nothing. It seemed
to the gardaí that he was discouraging cooperation with their
investigation. The next Sunday Fr Dowley told his congregation
that:

I have heard that I am going to be put in jail over telling the
people to keep their mouths shut about the case. Sure I never
said that to you. If I had any information to give I would give
it. I don't believe that story about the body being rolled up in a
blanket and thrown into a hole. There is something fishy about
it. The only proof they have of that is a fool of a fellow over in
Stradbally that denied it when he was sworn.

O'Mara was so concerned about Dowley's comments to his
congregation that he reported them to HQ and complained
about them to the bishop. He wrote that Fr Dowley was closely

connected with the Whelan family and he described him as 'a peculiar type of man anxious for opposition and desirous of earning for himself the name of martyr'.

However, Fr O'Shea, the curate in Ballylaneen, continued to be supportive of the investigation, as did the parish priest in Stradbally, Fr Lannon. The latter spoke at Sunday mass asking the community 'to do what they can in the interests of justice', and he was active among the people urging them to give any information to the gardaí which would lead to the discovery of the body.

People began to speak more freely to the gardaí about the stories and rumours they had heard. As already mentioned, one of these stories was that the body had originally been buried in the convent grounds but had been moved on 21 January. The body had then, according to one account, been buried in a garden on the farm of George Cummins, one of the accused men. The garden was carefully searched with spikes 'specially made and in such a way that they will bring back a portion of anything with which they come in contact' but nothing came of it. From another source came information that the body was in an artificial pond in the nearby Woodhouse estate. The gardaí dug a trench about twenty yards long from the pond to a nearby river to drain it, and then they carefully probed and searched the mud which was left behind, but again without result.

The secret garda exhumations and searches in local grave-yards were still being carried out. However, their cover was blown when local people in Ballylaneen spotted men in civilian clothes probing graves in the local cemetery early on a Sunday morning. Chief Superintendent O'Mara was reported in the newspapers as denying that any graves had been interfered with by the gardaí. 'Thus the mystery deepens,' wrote *The Irish Times*. 'On the one hand there is absolute evidence that graves have been interfered with, people in the locality have seen men enter the graveyards, and on the other hand, there is no explanation of the movements of these strangers.'

These newspaper reports drew a furious reprimand for O'Mara, this time from General O'Duffy himself:

Press interviews by members of the garda in connection with the disappearance of Laurence Griffin are strictly prohibited as from receipt of this minute.

My repeated verbal instructions to you in this matter have not been complied with, and the result is very damaging to the prestige of the Force. I must hold you responsible for any breach of my orders in this regard, and you will take the necessary steps to prevent a recurrence ...

It is absurd for a responsible Police officer to emphatically deny that we have examined certain graves when everyone in the area, and many outside it, are aware that we have been doing this for the past month. Why not keep silent? The latest mystery, as reported in yesterday's 'Independent', is becoming as involved as the first.

In his written account O'Mara denies that he spoke to the newspapers at all at this time, and blames the press men for misrepresenting him. This is unlikely, however, because O'Mara is quoted in several newspapers by different reporters as denying that the gardaí were interfering with graves. Journalists working on crime cases both in 1930 and today are dependent on the goodwill of the investigating guards for help and information. They would therefore be slow to deliberately alienate those very same gardaí by concocting fictitious interviews with them. The idea that two or more journalists simultaneously took this course of action is not believable.

The continuing failure to find the body and the looming humiliation of the prosecution case against the ten accused also weighed heavily against Chief Superintendent O'Mara with his superiors at garda HQ. General O'Duffy decided to take Chief Superintendent O'Mara off the case of the missing postman and place Superintendent Hunt in charge of it. To add insult to injury, Hunt was ordered to bypass O'Mara, the senior officer in the division, and to report directly to garda HQ, and O'Mara was ordered to provide whatever assistance was requested by the lower-ranking officer.

Chapter 15

⟡

The tension and excitement around Waterford courthouse was at fever pitch on Friday 7 March, for this was the day on which the prosecutor, Mr Finlay, had promised he would finally prove his case. The press men and public alike expected to hear dramatic new evidence that would at least prove that the accused persons had a case to answer and should be sent forward for a full jury trial. Once Justice McCabe had taken his seat, Mr Finlay rose and began to speak:

On last Saturday, when the case was before you, I asked for a remand so that further inquiries might be pursued. The police then had hope of finding the body. Those inquiries have taken place during the week, and so far have not proved successful. There would, in my view probably be evidence implicating some of the defendants but there is no doubt that it would be more satisfactory in the interests of justice if the body of Laurence Griffin were found. In these circumstances it will be necessary to pursue further inquiries in the case. It would not be fair to the prisoners that they should be further remanded, and in the circumstances I ask liberty to withdraw the charges entered in your book.

There was complete silence in the courtroom, as if those present could not quite believe what they were hearing, or had not fully absorbed the meaning of what had just been said. Looking towards counsel for the defence, Justice McCabe said: 'I do not suppose that there is any response on the other side?' The various defence counsels nodded their assent and Justice McCabe ordered that the case against the accused be thrown out. Then, to add further to the humiliation of the prosecution he stated:

> the only comment I want to make is that the prosecution has said that there is evidence to implicate some of the defendants. I say that nothing in the evidence put before me implicates any one of the defendants with any of the charges.

The judge then rose and proceeded to leave the courtroom. The whole proceeding had lasted less than five minutes. For a moment, the public and the accused persons themselves were stunned into silence. Then, suddenly, there was an outburst of applause and cheering. Dozens of friends and supporters rushed towards the dock to shake hands with the accused while others who could not get near them shouted their congratulations. The court cleared in a few minutes as the newly freed prisoners and their supporters made their way outside, where further noisy celebrations took place. 'Right will always prevail over might,' shouted Thomas Cashin exuberantly while James Whelan told a reporter: 'I was confident we would all be set free.'

Gardaí Dullea and Murphy were unable to join in the subsequent celebrations as they were ordered to report immediately to garda HQ and had to catch the next available train to Dublin. The rest of the released persons had lunch in a Waterford hotel. Later on the Whelans left for Stradbally, driven by their solicitor Peter O'Connor. The other accused men travelled back to Stradbally in another motor car, while their friends and supporters followed in the special bus which had been hired for the day. The *Cork Examiner* reporter witnessed the reunion of the school headmaster and his wife:

> Mrs Cashin was bringing her children back from the school, which they attended three miles away, and could be seen driving the little pony car down the long straggling roadway. As she approached her cottage she saw the men descending from the motor car. The children saw them too. 'Mummy, mummy, there's daddy,' they cried gleefully. Mrs Cashin could hardly believe it. She jumped from the trap and the next second was clasped in her husband's arms. Then came the children's turn. They clung to their father, and altogether laughing and crying as they entered their cottage.

The Whelans held court in their public house, receiving friends and visitors, while out in the square villagers clustered in groups and discussed the dramatic end to the case which had obsessed them for months.

The return of the Stradbally Ten to the village made life all the more difficult for Jim Fitzgerald. Even though he had gone back on his original accusations, it was his evidence, whether truthful or otherwise, which had caused ten of his neighbours to face the ordeal of imprisonment and murder charges. These ten had included some of the most powerful and influential people in Stradbally. Even apart from the headmaster and the Whelan family, several of the other accused were farmers who would have had a higher social status than Fitzgerald, a mere labourer, and who were the type of people who would formerly have given him employment. But nobody would give him work now, and he could not venture from his house without bumping into relatives or friends of those whom he had accused. Jim Fitzgerald was a social outcast.

Several days after the collapse of the case against the Stradbally Ten, Jim Fitzgerald disappeared from the district, fuelling further rumours and newspaper headlines such as: 'Mystery Takes New Turn – Disappearance of Witness'. The new sergeant in Stradbally, J. Mahoney, reported Fitzgerald as a missing person and asked that his description be circulated in garda bulletins. The request was passed up the line by Chief Superintendent O'Mara to garda HQ in Dublin. Their reply was that it was not the practice of An Garda Síochána to track the movements of migratory labourers. In fact the garda commissioner knew well where Jim Fitzgerald was. While one element in the force was treating him as a missing person, he had in fact been secretly spirited out of the district by the new head of the investigation, Superintendent Hunt.

After the collapse of the court case and his appointment in charge of the investigation, Superintendent Hunt had interviewed Jim Fitzgerald on two occasions. Hunt reported that Fitzgerald was in a state of terror, that he had been threatened repeatedly since the release of the prisoners, and that he could obtain no employment. In order to gain Fitzgerald's cooperation, Hunt organised employment for him with a farmer in Galway, where Hunt himself was normally based. Fitzgerald promised Hunt that he would tell him all he knew once he was far away from Stradbally. On Friday 14 March 1930, Fitzgerald packed some belongings in a bundle, informed Mrs Corbett that she could keep all the property he had left behind him in the house, told her he was leaving Stradbally for good, and was then driven away in a car, as we now know, by members of An Garda Síochána. Superintendent Hunt kept garda HQ informed of this operation but it was kept secret from Chief Superintendent O'Mara and most of the local force.

On Sunday 16 March Superintendent Hunt travelled to Galway and over the next two days Fitzgerald finally told him what seems to be a truthful account of what he knew about the disappearance of Larry Griffin. Fitzgerald now stated that he arrived at Whelan's pub between 7.30 p.m. and 8 p.m. on Christmas night. He was by himself and went to the back door at which he knocked. He was answered by Mary Jack Hannigan from the kitchen. He asked her to open the door but she at first refused. Eventually she unbolted the door and admitted him. Fitzgerald sat in the outer kitchen and after a few minutes James Whelan came in and at Fitzgerald's request he brought a bottle of stout from the bar. At about 8 p.m., while Fitzgerald was still in Whelan's kitchen, he saw Garda Dullea and Larry Griffin walk through a passage off the kitchen and go towards the yard. After a few minutes Dullea and Griffin returned from the yard and walked back up the passageway towards the pub. That was the last time Fitzgerald saw Larry Griffin.

At about 8.20 p.m. Fitzgerald left Whelan's kitchen and went outside where he met Thomas Corbett, Jim Murphy and Patrick Cunningham. They remained at Whelan's corner until about 9 p.m. and while there were supplied with a drink, through the hall door, by Cissie Whelan. At about 9 p.m. they saw Sergeant Cullinane and Guard Frawley pass on patrol and immediately afterwards Fitzgerald, Murphy, Cunningham and Corbett went to O'Reilly's public house where they had more drink. They left O'Reilly's about 9.30 p.m. and went to the hall where they remained until 11 p.m. when the row occurred between Thomas Corbett and William Cleary. Guard Frawley entered the hall as the row was in progress and he separated

Corbett and Cleary. After that Fitzgerald, Corbett and Cunningham left the hall together. Cunningham parted from them outside the door as his route home was different from theirs. Fitzgerald and Corbett, who resided in the same house, went straight home and Fitzgerald was positive that Corbett did not go back to Stradbally again that night. Fitzgerald went to bed immediately when he got home.

Fitzgerald now said that it was Corbett who had told him the whole story about Larry being killed in Whelan's pub a few days after Christmas. Corbett had heard the story from the farmer Patrick Cunningham, for whom he was working at that time. Instead of going home after parting company with them at the hall on Christmas night, Patrick Cunningham had gone to Whelan's pub, where he had witnessed the row and Larry's death sometime between 11 p.m. and 11.30 p.m. Corbett did not mention anything to Fitzgerald about Ballinasisla or Tankardstown mineshafts or about the blanket, the half-hundred weight or Cashin's car. It was subsequently from different sources that Fitzgerald heard about these elements of the story, apart from the blanket, which he stated was a pure invention of his own after one of the guards who were taking his statement suggested that the body must have been wrapped up in something.

Hunt was satisfied that Fitzgerald was now telling the truth. We can be certain that this new account was much closer to the truth than Fitzgerald's original statement, because it is consistent with the evidence of other witnesses that he had a drink on the street outside Whelan's, that he went to O'Reilly's pub, and that he was later in the hall where he witnessed the fight between William Cleary and Thomas Corbett. It is credible that Fitzgerald heard most of the account of what happened in Whelan's that night from Corbett, and that he picked up other details from other sources, for similar versions of this story were in wide circulation in the district at the time, and were clearly believed by the locals to be the truth of what had happened.

All this goes a long way towards explaining how Fitzgerald may have come to give his original statement to the gardaí. The fact that Fitzgerald was a country labourer of limited education would have made it seem unlikely to the investigating gardaí that he invented his original statement. This made them all the more susceptible to believing him. However, Fitzgerald did not need to 'invent' the story, for he had heard detailed and vivid accounts of Larry's death in Whelan's pub from Corbett and from other sources. Fitzgerald may not have seen this as 'lying' because, aside from the fact that he himself was not present, he believed that the events had happened exactly as he described them.

As we have seen, the gardaí were under huge pressure to uncover the truth of the story, and they in turn brought this pressure to bear on those they were interviewing. Even Chief Superintendent O'Mara in his own account writes about questioning witnesses '*very* hard' and, as we will see in a later chapter, we know for certain that another witness was physically tortured. We also know from Fitzgerald that he was asked at least some leading questions, such as the comment by one of the interrogators that the body must have been wrapped up in something. To a labourer such as Fitzgerald, any garda would have been a figure of authority and greater social standing than himself. The fact that Chief Superintendent O'Mara was interviewing him would have been all the more intimidating, and it is not hard to imagine how Fitzgerald might have wanted to please them by telling them what they wanted to know and were predisposed to believe. This would also have given Fitzgerald a temporary and intoxicating sense of importance and, in the heat of the moment, he would not have thought through all the consequences of his actions.

In spite of the collapse of the case against Gardaí Dullea and Murphy, General O'Duffy had decided that the time had come to throw them and the other original Stradbally gardaí out of the force. The disciplinary case against them, as summarised by Superintendent Hunt, was damning:

As will be seen from a study of the statements made by the guards themselves there was gross indiscipline at Stradbally on 25 December. The barrack orderly Guard Sullivan, failed to keep a true record in the Station Diary and there was much drinking of intoxicants on the part of the Guards. The patrols were not performed as it was represented they had been and the entries made by Guard Murphy in the patrol [book] were obviously untrue. In many other respects the action of the Garda in connection with the inquiry into the disappearance of Larry Griffin was subversive of all order or discipline. Guard Dullea concealed the fact that he had accompanied Griffin, who was undoubtedly drunk, outside Stradbally on the night he disappeared and Sergeant Cullinane when he learned of this also failed to report it to his officers although he must have been aware at the time their inquiries were directed to ascertaining who was the last person known to have been in Griffin's company. In short, the statements made by the Gardaí contradict one another and are undoubtedly a tissue of falsehoods. No reliance can be placed on the word of such men. The action of Guard Dullea in warning Mrs Frawley (wife of Guard Frawley) and her sister not to say that they saw him and Larry Griffin together on Christmas night is little short of disclosing a criminal intent.

On 24 April 1930 the entire original Stradbally garda party were dismissed from the force.

Deputy Commissioner Coogan, however, also had Chief Superintendent O'Mara in his sights. He wrote a memo in late March to General O'Duffy arguing that it was also necessary to take disciplinary action against O'Mara and Superintendent Keenan for the state of affairs which had prevailed in Stradbally barracks on Christmas Day 1929. Keenan was in charge of the Tramore garda district in which Stradbally was located, and O'Mara was in charge of the entire Waterford division. Coogan told O'Duffy that 'indiscipline would be too mild a term' for the state of affairs in Stradbally barracks at Christmas 1929 and that 'anarchy reigned supreme' there. It was 'quite apparent that the party had nothing to fear' from either Chief Superintendent O'Mara or Superintendent Keenan. O'Mara was also blamed, as we will see in the next chapter, for the use of strong-arm methods against one of the witnesses in the course of the investigation. General O'Duffy agreed with Deputy Commissioner Coogan's recommendation. At the beginning of April 1930 Superintendent Keenan was told he was to be transferred to Newport, County Tipperary, and a few weeks later Chief Superintendent O'Mara was ordered to transfer to Letterkenny, County Donegal.

O'Mara's account written years later reveals the depth of his bitterness at his treatment:

> I was very downhearted and crestfallen not so because I felt that I had been unjustly but unmistakably saddled for all time, as far as the public were concerned, with all the odium which the failure of the case, the third degree methods and the other bungling, known publicly, deserved but because I believed that my transfer at that time suggested, and was deliberately intended to suggest to the public, that the bunglings were far more serious and far more numerous than was known outside official circles. In any

case my experiences had driven me, rightly or wrongly, to the firm conviction that vanity and treachery overshadowed justice and manliness in the majority of the Headquarters Staff of that period and that many officers outside that Staff were prepared to sacrifice as a mere trifle the career of any officer in order to pander to that vanity and treachery. In those circumstances I had to plough a lonely furrow and regard everybody with very profound suspicion. It is hard for a person who hasn't experience of such an existence to picture what a terrible thing it is.

In his account O'Mara stated that he had to send two of his children, aged five and eight years, away to boarding school due to the impossibility of obtaining suitable lodgings in Letterkenny and that his wife, his two-year-old daughter and himself had to live in a hotel room for four months. He wrote that HQ were aware of his difficulties but that they refused him permission to live away from Letterkenny where it might have been easier to find a house, and he believed this was intended as a further punishment.

Chapter 16

Between 26 and 28 February 1930 lawyers acting on behalf of Tommy Corbett served summonses on four of the investigating officers in the missing postman case, claiming damages for false imprisonment, assault, threats to murder him and bodily harm. The officers against whom the allegations were being made were Inspector McNamara and Detective Gardaí Driscoll, Gantley and O'Rourke. Corbett claimed the assaults took place when he was brought in for questioning a second time on 6 February, a fortnight after he and Jim Fitzgerald had given their initial statements to the gardaí. At the time the summonses were served the ten accused were being held on remand in Ballybricken prison and the hearings in Waterford district court were still ongoing.

When the case opened in the high court in Dublin on 3 December 1930 the details of Corbett's allegations were made known as follows: Inspector McNamara and the three detectives had at first tried to bribe Corbett into saying that he was in Whelan's pub on Christmas night and they offered him £150 and a good job in Ford's motor-car factory to corroborate Jim

Fitzgerald's statement. However, Corbett had told them that if he got £50,000 he could not tell them he was in Whelan's that night, because it was not true. When he refused to cooperate they threatened him, and said that if he did not give the evidence they wanted he would disappear as Griffin had and that they would bring him to Ballinasisla mineshaft and throw him down 'beside Larry'. After a while they forced him into a motor car and drove him to the cliffs at Bunmahon. They brought him to the edge of the cliffs and threatened to throw him over into the sea if he did not say that he was in Whelan's public house on Christmas night. Inspector McNamara then caught him by the throat and collar of the coat, saying that he (Corbett) was in Whelan's on Christmas night. Detective Driscoll drew a revolver from his pocket and shoved the barrel into the side of Corbett's mouth, threatening to shoot him if he did not give them the evidence they wanted. When he was finally brought back to the barracks at 5.30 a.m. in the morning he was ordered to go home and remain silent about the treatment which he had received. Mrs Corbett gave evidence that when her husband returned from the barracks he looked frightened and that his coat was torn.

The defendants denied all of Corbett's allegations. They claimed that he attended the barracks for questioning voluntarily and that he could have left at any time if he had wanted to. The defence also suggested that Corbett was not the real person who was bringing this action, but that it was, in fact, financed by the Whelans as a means of blighting any evidence that might be obtained in connection with the disappearance of Larry Griffin. Mr Woods, representing the defendants, alleged that Corbett was 'only a gramophone for the Whelans', and that the case was a 'try on'.

Mr Justice Hanna, during his address to the jury, certainly could not have been accused of showing bias against the gardaí. He described the difficulty in obtaining information about the postman's disappearance 'as a disgrace to the country' and said that everybody around Stradbally had 'closed up like an oyster':

> It is a disgraceful state of affairs that public spirit should be so low that when a poor man in a humble position like Griffin disappeared under suspicious circumstances all those in the neighbourhood, for what reason I can only surmise, closed their mouths and declined to give the police any assistance, obviously with the object of protecting someone. I am not saying for a moment that Mr Corbett is in this category, but you do have to consider what the motive behind this case is. The defendants were active agents of the state investigating the mystery of Laurence Griffin's disappearance, and it has been suggested that the action has been brought against them to prevent them from ever being in a position to hold up their heads before a jury and give evidence that a jury would accept, because it is perfectly obvious that if they are found liable in this action their reputation will be so blighted that probably no jury would be inclined to accept any testimony that they would give. You will have to

consider whether this action could be explained by a motive of that kind.

In spite of the questions raised in Justice Hanna's summing up, the jury believed Tommy Corbett's allegations and awarded him damages of £500, plus costs which amounted to almost another £500, bringing the total to £1,000, an astronomical sum in 1930, when a decent three-bedroom cottage could be bought for about £175.

The mistreatment of Tommy Corbett was not the first such incident to occur in Waterford. After the killings of two gardaí by the IRA in 1926, republican prisoners who were in custody on totally unconnected charges were beaten in their cells for hours by both uniformed gardaí and detectives. The officers involved in that affair were subsequently dismissed on the orders of the Minister for Justice. The garda files on the missing postman case show that from an early stage General O'Duffy and Deputy Commissioner Coogan believed the allegations of assault by Tommy Corbett to be true, and that they held Chief Superintendent O'Mara responsible for them. Deputy Commissioner Coogan wrote that many 'of the gardaí in Waterford division and perhaps in other divisions have strong suspicions of what happened, if they indeed are not aware of the facts'. General O'Duffy wrote the following stern warning to Chief Superintendent O'Mara on 5 March 1930:

I must again warn you against the adoption of anything in the nature of third degree methods when interviewing suspects or witnesses. I have made this very clear to you at Conferences held in the Depot on 30 and 31 January last in connection with the Stradbally case. Criminal investigations must be carried out strictly in accordance with the Regulations and any departure therefrom will not be tolerated. You are held responsible for the acts of your subordinates in this matter. If we cannot succeed without resorting to objectionable methods then we must accept failure.

O'Mara, in his account written some years after the events, also accepts that the men under his command assaulted Corbett. Along with the state of anarchy which had existed in Stradbally barracks when Larry Griffin disappeared, and the failure of the case in the district court, the mistreatment of Tommy Corbett was yet another factor in O'Mara's removal from the case and his eventual transfer to Donegal. However, according to O'Mara's version of events, he was made a scapegoat for these failures, when it was in fact General O'Duffy himself and Deputy Commissioner Coogan who were responsible.

O'Mara's account builds up a picture in which General O'Duffy and Deputy Commissioner Coogan tolerated and encouraged the use of strong-arm methods in the missing postman investigation. We have already seen how O'Mara alleged that Deputy Commissioner Coogan had personally beaten members of the original Stradbally garda party while interrogating them in the garda depot. O'Mara also claimed that he had prevented Detective Gardaí O'Rourke and Driscoll from 'beating the truth' out of the witness John Power, after the deputy commissioner had ordered them to do so. It is impossible at this stage to prove or disprove these allegations.

In relation to the mistreatment of Tommy Corbett, O'Mara claims that, at the conference held at Waterford garda station on 4 February 1930 when Inspector McNamara had just arrived from Cork, General O'Duffy told McNamara that Corbett knew all about Griffin's death and where the body was and that McNamara was to get the information out of him before the district court hearing so that there would be corroboration of Jim Fitzgerald's statement. According to O'Mara, the exact words O'Duffy used were: 'Tommy Corbett knows all about the case. I want you to get it out of him any way.' In other words, according to O'Mara, it was the garda commissioner himself who gave the green light for the use of strong-arm methods in the questioning of Tommy Corbett. For many years, O'Mara's version of events was the only one available to anyone interested in researching the case of the missing postman.

However, the garda files made available as a result of the RTÉ *CSÍ* documentary about the case of the missing postman cast serious doubt on O'Mara's version of events. These files show that, a few days after Tommy Corbett's summonses were served on the four officers, O'Mara wrote to garda HQ to say that he had investigated the allegations and had found them to be without foundation. He gave a detailed account of all that had transpired the night that Corbett was brought in for questioning, emphasising the voluntary and friendly nature of the proceedings. He also attempted to discredit Corbett by drawing attention to his involvement with the anti-Treaty forces during the Civil War. He wrote that Corbett 'had to marry his wife' and that he and his family were 'of disreputable character'. However, in his later account, O'Mara conveniently omits to mention this vigorous defence that he himself had made of the four officers. The idea that O'Mara wrote to Coogan and O'Duffy to deny the very occurrence of garda brutality which he knew General O'Duffy had given the go-ahead for is not believable.

One possibility is that O'Mara genuinely did not believe at the time that the brutality had taken place under his own nose, and that his later account was an attempt to whitewash his own lack of knowledge and control regarding the men under his command. The other possibility is that O'Mara did know at the time of the brutality, perhaps having instigated it himself, and that he conspired with the officers involved to hide it from his own superiors. This is certainly what Deputy Commissioner Coogan believed at the time. Upon receipt of O'Mara's report, Coogan wrote to General O'Duffy that the 'chief superintendent's implicit faith in the members concerned and his firm conviction that they did not ill-treat Corbett in any way is about the most surprising piece of cold-blooded lying that has ever come to my knowledge'. Whatever the truth of the matter, it is clear that there is a certain rewriting of history going on in O'Mara's account, in an attempt to redeem his own reputation. O'Mara's lack of credibility on the issue of Corbett's mistreatment must also cast doubt over his other allegations of misconduct against General O'Duffy and Deputy Commissioner Coogan.

The position of Inspector McNamara, and of Detectives Driscoll, O'Rourke and Gantley as members of An Garda Síochána, was clearly untenable after they had been found by the high court to have beaten a witness. The government demanded that they be dismissed from the force, although interestingly General O'Duffy resisted, perhaps believing that the blame for the events lay with their superior officer Chief Superintendent O'Mara, and that they had just been carrying out orders. O'Duffy was overruled, although the government did accede to his request that the men be allowed the fig leaf of resigning of their own accord, rather than being officially dismissed. Given the choice between dismissal and resignation, all four men chose the latter course of action.

In theory, Tommy Corbett was now a very rich man. However, it was one thing for the courts to award damages – it was another thing altogether to actually collect them. There followed many months of to-ing and fro-ing between various interested parties as they pursed their conflicting agendas. The four ex-gardaí wanted to settle the claim on more favourable terms than the £1,000 awarded against them by the court. In 1930 the annual salary of a detective garda was about £200 and a garda inspector would have earned about £300. Even if the ex-gardaí had still had their salaries, the award would have exceeded their combined yearly income. But now that they had been thrown out of the force, it is probable that they were simply unable to raise the money. They started trying to negotiate directly with Corbett, rather than through his solicitor, and tried to tempt him to settle for cash in hand. Even a portion of the £500 would have been a huge sum to a poor labourer like Tommy Corbett, and as the months wore on and there was no sign of his money he was more inclined to believe that half a loaf was better than none at all. However, his solicitor Peter O'Connor was furious with Corbett for going behind his back, and was worried that a settlement between Corbett and the four gardaí might leave him without his legal costs. Most interestingly of all, Thomas Cashin, Patrick Whelan and some of the other former defendants kept getting involved in the affair, trying to discourage Corbett from settling the case directly with the four ex-gardaí. Cashin and the others seemed to be worried that the unpredictable Corbett might make a deal with the ex-guards that would involve him revealing what he knew about Christmas night and the fate of the postman.

There are many pages of notes in the garda files which reveal that the gardaí were keeping a close eye on these developments and gathering as much intelligence as possible about them. The four ex-gardaí met with Thomas Corbett without his solicitor at Tramore on 3 September 1931 in their efforts to get him to accept a settlement. When Corbett was passing through Stradbally village, having returned from Tramore, Thomas Cashin called him into his house. Later on, when Corbett had left Cashin's house, the schoolteacher was then seen entering Whelan's. Then again on 5 September Cashin went to visit Corbett. According to the garda notes there was 'great uneasiness amongst the Whelan and Cashin crowd' as a result of the contacts between Corbett and the ex-gardaí. That night, according to the garda notes, when John Fitzsimmons, a trusted friend of the Whelans, entered the pub he found Patrick Whelan crying:

> Fitzsimmons conversed with him and said what was the need for worry now, that sure everything was passed and gone and the whole thing was dead, and that the answer Whelan made was that it was only now things were starting properly.

When Tommy Corbett had met the ex-gardaí in Tramore he had been unemployed but, all of a sudden, he received employment from John Cunningham, a brother of Patrick Cunningham (who had been in Whelan's on Christmas night, and who had subsequently been one of the ten persons arrested and charged in relation to Larry Griffin's disappearance), even though, according to the garda notes, Cunningham 'did not want a man because his holding is very small'.

At about 9 p.m. on the night of 18 September 1931 solicitor Peter O'Connor called to see Tommy Corbett. As he passed through the village both Thomas Cashin and John Cunningham followed him to Corbett's home. A sister-in-law of Tommy Corbett later told local people that Peter O'Connor asked Corbett at this meeting:

> why didn't the ex-detective officers go to his office to settle and that Tommy said that a detective officer or a guard would never darken his door again and that at that remark Mr O'Connor got into a furious rage and said he'd have satisfaction.

What is most interesting about this incident is that, according to the source of the story, Thomas Cashin intervened to try to make peace between Corbett and his solicitor. Cashin was clearly doing all he could to prevent Corbett from falling out with his solicitor and making some sort of deal directly with the ex-detectives.

At 1 a.m. the next morning a car was seen passing through the village coming from Corbett's house and then at 8 a.m. the same morning ex-Garda O'Rourke was seen passing by Corbett's house in a motor car. According to the garda notes:

> Immediately everybody started making enquiries and the rumour

spread that the ex-detectives had Corbett away during the night and that they arrived at a settlement and then drove him home. This rumour caused the greatest trouble amongst Whelan and Cashin crowd, etc., and the whole of them were aroused and moved in all directions. It was easy to notice all the excitement that prevailed.

That night a local man, Johnnie Gleeson, asked Sergeant O'Connor of Stradbally garda barracks to go for a walk with him. As they were walking Gleeson expressed the opinion that Whelan, Cashin and company were afraid that Corbett was 'capable of anything' and that 'they wanted to close his mouth'. Gleeson also told the sergeant 'that Whelan and Cashin were killed for to get information and that they could not get it as the Corbett men and women had refused to give any'. The sergeant wrote in his report of the conversation that Gleeson:

> felt very disturbed and mentioned that Corbett was a dangerous man and on a few occasions he said that he hoped the detective officers would not settle with that fellow, that we had queer law if they should give money to the likes of him.

The next day according to the garda notes, Sunday 20 September, the Corbetts disclosed that Tommy had agreed to settle with the ex-detective officers and that he was to get the money on 22 September:

> The news took Whelan, Cashin, Cunninghams [*sic*], etc., by
> surprise and nothing but excitement prevailed and they moved,
> rushed, and conversed so much with each other that the people
> of the village could not help watching them. Opinions were
> expressed openly that the end was near at hand for that once
> Corbett had the money that he would disclose all that happened
> at Whelans Christmas Night 1929.

It was reported that Tommy Corbett had been heard saying to a local man that 'he could make Whelans as small as a box of matches'.

However, it is evident that Corbett's plan to settle directly with the former detectives was vigorously opposed by his solicitor Peter O'Connor when he heard about it. On 21 September Corbett told Sergeant O'Connor of Stradbally barracks that:

> Peter O'Connor was in a terrible rage because he [Corbett] was
> settling with the detective officers and that he [O'Connor] swore
> that he should get the costs of the case and that if Corbett settled
> with them that he [Corbett] should pay the costs.

Corbett told the sergeant he feared that if he did settle with the ex-gardaí 'that O'Connor might claim the expenses with the result that he would have him [Corbett] in gaol for the remainder of his life'. Corbett said:

that he didn't know what he would do but that if he thought that O'Connor could not claim costs from him that he would settle in five minutes with the detective officers and that five minutes after he would not stay in Stradbally.

The sergeant tried to take advantage of the conversation with Corbett to probe him about the events of Christmas night 1929 in Whelan's public house, but Corbett denied being on the premises that night. The sergeant wrote that he pushed Corbett pretty hard about the matter:

> He was in agreement with me that it was an accident and that they did the wrong thing, etc., but once he saw that I was going a little too far for his taste he began to deny all knowledge then.

The following morning the solicitor Peter O'Connor's car collected Tommy Corbett and his wife and brought them to O'Connor's office in Waterford. The solicitor was facing a heavy loss over the work he had put into the case. He was dealing with an unreliable client in Tommy Corbett, as Corbett had come very close to making a direct settlement with the four ex-gardaí behind his back, and without any regard for the solicitor's expenses. He therefore offered to buy out Corbett's claim for damages for the sum of £125, on the condition that Corbett would have no further dealings with the ex-gardaí. For the solicitor this had the advantage of getting rid of Corbett and forcing the ex-gardaí to deal directly with him, if they were to clear their legal obligations. For Corbett, it meant cash in hand without the prospect of O'Connor pursuing him for costs, and he jumped at the offer. And for Cashin, the Whelans and the Cunninghams, it meant that Corbett would keep his mouth shut about what really happened on Christmas night.

As soon as Corbett returned to the village, the celebrations began. Thomas Cashin welcomed him back and then accompanied Corbett and his wife into Whelan's. Having spent some time in the public house, Cashin drove Corbett and his wife home and Cashin was observed shaking hands with Corbett and saying to him: 'You were always a man Tommy and you have proved yourself a man now.' The Cunninghams and some of the other former defendants visited the Corbetts that night 'and there was whiskey and stout in plenty there' according to garda intelligence. And while Corbett fell out with his own relatives shortly afterwards when he refused to share his windfall with them, that was of no concern to Cashin, the Whelans and the Cunninghams, for they were quite confident now that Corbett would not be speaking up about the events of Christmas night.

Chapter 17

It seemed to the farmers around Stradbally in 1930 as if spring would never arrive after the terrible winter they had endured. Heavy rains and harsh winds still prevailed, conditions which retarded growth and impeded outdoor farm work. Little progress could be made with spring-seeding operations and cattle and sheep were in a poorer condition than they had been at the same time the year before. Meanwhile Superintendent Hunt was pursuing the renewed investigation into Larry Griffin's disappearance. His reports reveal a difference in style and approach from Chief Superintendent O'Mara's original investigation. There were fewer formal interviews – Hunt favoured methods such as befriending and recruiting local people to assist in intelligence gathering and making deductions from observations of people's movements.

For example, on 12 March 1930 Superintendent Hunt reported to Deputy Commissioner Coogan that he had been 'concentrating on securing the services of some trustworthy civilians who would take a genuine interest in securing information as to the whereabouts of the body'. He also reported that he had spent two hours with the local curate, Fr Burke, on the previous Sunday. It was dark when Hunt left the priest's house and within fifteen minutes Fr Burke was observed 'stealing by the wall' and entering Thomas Cashin's house where he remained for some time. Hunt had 'heard since that he told Cashin everything I said'. The superintendent was convinced that Fr Burke had either been present in Whelan's pub when Griffin met his death or else that he was called to attend him before he died. He described Fr Burke as a rogue and a more 'cunning rascal' than he had met in his life.

In mid-April the weather finally turned, much to the relief of the farming community. The conditions were dry and favourable for tillage operations and considerable headway was made with all fieldwork. Most of the grain and potato crops were sown before the end of the month and milk yields started to increase.

Superintendent Hunt believed that he too was making headway and that a breakthrough in the case was imminent. He reported that his latest enquiries had led him to believe that the body of the missing postman was buried in a tillage field not far from Stradbally convent's grounds. He told HQ that he had 'received absolutely reliable information to this effect and our informant hopes in a short time to be able to point out the exact location of the body'. However, there was no further reference to this lead in subsequent reports available in the garda files and it is evident that nothing came of it.

Then again, at the beginning of May, Hunt reported 'persistent rumours' that the postman's body had originally been buried in the grounds of Stradbally convent, but that it had subsequently been moved to the Glen Bog after the searches of the bog had finished. Hunt told HQ that he believed this information came from reliable sources and he attached so much importance to it that he contemplated organising a search party. However, the arrival back from Dublin in February of the dismissed Gardaí Frawley, Sullivan, Dullea and Murphy influenced Hunt to hold off on the search and await further developments.

Dullea and Murphy stayed in Whelan's for three nights, after which both men left Stradbally for their native districts – Ballineen in County Cork in the case of Dullea and Bruree in County Limerick in the case of Murphy. Both Frawley and Sullivan visited Whelan's frequently during those days and they saw Dullea and Murphy off at Durrow station when they were leaving for home. On his return from the train station on Tuesday evening, Frawley called at the barracks looking for Superintendent Hunt, and on being informed that the latter was in O'Reilly's public house he followed him there. Hunt gave an account of their conversation in a report to garda HQ:

> He asked me for a private interview and on going with him to a private room he asked me what I would do for him if he helped to get Griffin's body. My reply was that I could not promise anything until I knew what help he was prepared to give. He then

said he would do his utmost and that he hoped I would get him
a job if he succeeded. He added he did not want re-instatement
in the guards. Ultimately I promised I would find him as good a
job as the guards if he kept his word.

On Thursday 1 May Garda Sullivan's wife came to the barracks
looking for a Detective Garda Hanley and asked him to come
back to her home with her to talk to her husband. When
Detective Hanley arrived at Sullivan's house, he was met there
not just by Garda Sullivan, but by Garda Frawley also. According
to Hunt's report, both Sullivan and Frawley asked Hanley what
guarantee they would get if they helped in putting the body of
Larry Griffin into the hands of the gardaí, and on being told by
him that they would be reinstated in the guards or get a better
job they promised to have the body inside a week.

On 2 May, according to Hunt's report, Mrs Frawley called
on Detective Hanley and told him that her husband had
been speaking to Ned Morrissey the previous night, and that
Morrissey had told him that Larry Griffin's body was in the
Glen Bog 'with his bag, baggage, uniform and all'. Mrs Frawley
told Hunt that her husband had promised to get Morrissey to
go with him to the bog that very night to point out the spot
where the body was buried. Garda Sullivan was also trying
to prove his good intentions to Hunt by hanging out with
Morrissey to see if he could pick up any information from him.
Hunt wrote to headquarters:

I am firmly convinced that Frawley is fully conversant with everything that happened Griffin up to the last removal of his body. He may not be aware of Griffin's final resting place but this is the only part of the proceedings he is unacquainted with. At the moment Frawley and Sullivan have only about £2 each between them ... and they have no prospects whatever of getting employment and I think we may regard their efforts to help now as genuine.

In considering the information regarding the final burial of Larry Griffin's body in the Glen Bog, Hunt felt that Patrick Whelan's letter from prison some months earlier advising a search of the bog was also significant:

I have given this aspect of the question much thought during the past week and I have come to the conclusion that Whelan was then afraid someone in the crowd would 'split' and he wrote the letters giving a sort of general hint about the bog so that in the event of the body being found there he could always claim to have been the first to give the information. This would be consistent with Whelan's mentality. In the interview I had with Whelan he stoutly maintained the body was in the bog but never ever suggested Griffin wandered in there. In two interviews Sergeant O'Connor of this station had with him since his attitude was the same and it is this conduct of Whelan's that makes me think all the more of the information we have been receiving lately.

As Hunt was writing his report on 2 May he hoped that Frawley and Morrissey would go to the bog that very night, that they would be followed and watched discreetly by his men, and that, if the body of Larry Griffin was subsequently found at the spot where they would be seen to halt, it would be material evidence against them. Again, however, the garda files are silent on what happened afterwards; whether or not Frawley and Morrissey did go to the bog that night, we know that nothing new emerged as a result.

Around this time Miss Orpen, a young woman who resided at Kilminnion near Stradbally, gave the gardaí some new information. At the time of Larry Griffin's disappearance she was being courted by James Whelan, the son of the publican. On Christmas night Miss Orpen and her sister were visiting an aunt in Stradbally and they left for home at about 8.40 p.m. Their route home went past Whelan's, up the Chapel Road and past the Five Crossroads. James Whelan was evidently watching out for their departure and joined them on their way. He told Miss Orpen that his mother had done her best to make him go home with Larry Griffin but that he did not want to miss spending the night in her company. He told her that he had said to his mother 'let the guards leave him at home'. Owing to pressure from her relatives Miss Orpen had latterly severed her relations with James Whelan, and it seemed that this explained her coming forward with information at this late stage.

On 15 May Superintendent Hunt reported yet another apparently promising source of intelligence:

During the past week Garda Leary of Leamybrien established very friendly relations with a man named Byrne and his wife who formerly resided in Stradbally but now reside in Dungarvan. The Byrnes were bitter irregulars and the man had been interned for quite a long time. When they were residing in Stradbally Mrs Byrne and the Whelan girls, particularly Cissie, were on very good terms. The latter used to tell all her secrets to Mrs Byrne, even not concealing the most intimate relations she had with Dullea. It has now been arranged by Mrs Byrne to invite Cissie to Dungarvan to stay with her for a few days and Cissie has agreed to go there on Tuesday next. There is good reason to believe that before the visit terminates Mrs Byrne may learn a good deal. Both herself and her husband have promised to do what they can in the matter. She states that she met Cissie on a few occasions since Christmas but only on one occasion was the subject of Larry's disappearance drawn down. Cissie then told Mrs Byrne that it was in the guards barrack that Larry died. It may be possible Cissie knows where the body is at present and Byrne and his wife are to concentrate on getting everything she does know from her.

The story that Larry Griffin died in Stradbally garda station was to crop up frequently from then on in the garda files, in local folklore and even, on occasion, in the press. According to one version of this story, Larry Griffin, suffering from the effects of too much alcohol, was brought by Gardaí Dullea and Murphy to the garda barracks, and put to bed in an upstairs room. However, having been left there, Griffin woke up, wandered out onto the landing and died after falling down the stairs, after which his death was covered up and his body disposed of.

Cissie Whelan did indeed visit her friend Mrs Byrne in Dungarvan, but only for a short time, and apparently Mrs Byrne did not have the opportunity to glean any more information from her. As with Superintendent Hunt's previous schemes for a breakthrough in the case, it seems that in the end nothing came of this plan.

Chapter 18

———◆———

When General Eoin O'Duffy opened his copy of the *Irish Independent* on 22 May 1930, he was surprised to see the following article:

MYSTERIOUS MEN IN DEMESNE

MISSING POSTMAN

WOMAN SEES STRANGE LIGHTS

An extraordinary story, stated to have been told by an ex-soldier named O'Brien has led to further searches by the civic guards for the body of Laurence Griffin, the Kilmacthomas postman who disappeared from Stradbally on Christmas Day. According to O'Brien, who lived in the gate lodge at the entrance to Woodhouse Demesne on the outskirts of Stradbally, shortly after midnight on December 28 he was disturbed by the rattling of the gate at the entrance to the demesne, and peeping through a window he saw between fifteen and twenty men carrying what appeared to be a

209

heavy body which they seemed to be endeavouring to conceal. He did not follow the matter up, but observed that the men proceeded in the direction of Ballyvoile Cliffs. The Civic Guards are now searching the demesne and cliffs.

A curious story is told by Mrs O'Sullivan, who lived close to the village of Stradbally. When she was returning from a visit to a friend's house on last Sunday about midnight she saw three lights hovering over a hedge on the roadside. Behind the lights she saw the figure of a man. She ran back to the village and aroused the Civic Guards. It is stated that a detective, who accompanied her to the place also saw the lights which disappeared almost immediately. No trace of a man was found.

Deputy Commissioner Coogan immediately contacted Superintendent Hunt and asked him to comment on the article. Hunt assured Coogan that there was very little truth in it:

It is more than a fortnight since I first heard the rumour about O'Brien's wife having seen men carrying the dead body of a man through Woodhouse gate and into the demesne and I immediately questioned herself and her husband but both emphatically denied having seen anything of the kind or having mentioned such subject to anybody. I further questioned a son of theirs Larry O'Brien from whom I took a written statement ... but he denied having ever heard his father or mother speak of such a thing. There is no truth whatever in the statement about the Guards searching Ballyvoile cliffs.

I have paid several visits to Woodhouse recently interviewing workmen and this may have given rise to the idea that we were searching there for the body.

Regarding the ghostly story about the mysterious lights and unidentified man, the truth was rather less sensational. At 12.45 a.m. on 15 May Detective Officer Gantley and Garda Twamley were halted on the road about 300 yards from Stradbally village by a Mrs Curran and her son, a boy of about twelve years of age, who informed them there was a light and what appeared to be a man's body lying against the ditch further down the road. The woman was in a very excited condition but eventually agreed to return and point out the object to the officers. On reaching the spot she pointed to the 'body' and said: 'There it is.' On examination it proved to be a phosphorescent light probably caused by a glow worm. Nearby was a decayed stump of an old tree and this may have caused the impression in her mind that there was the body of a man there. Rumours about ghosts, especially Larry Griffin's ghost, being seen in and around Stradbally were in daily circulation at this time, and it seems that these had an effect on Mrs Curran's imagination. Whatever the veracity of such stories, they made good copy for the newspapers.

Also around 22 May 1930, Superintendent Hunt had a long interview with ex-Garda Frawley, which he reported on to HQ:

At the outset of the interview he [ex-Garda Frawley] made a pretence of believing that nothing happened to Larry but towards the conclusion of the interview he was in a different mood but maintained his own innocence stoutly. He promised to do everything in his power to help find the body after getting a promise that his name would not be mentioned if he furnished information. Four or five days later his wife called at the barracks and asked for Detective Officer Hanley stating her husband wanted to see him. Detective Garda Hanley was not then in barracks but on his return about an hour later he went to Frawley's house only to be told by Frawley that he was sorry for sending for him and that he could not now tell him what he had intended to say to him. After some pressure by Hanley, Frawley said that the theory held by the authorities about Larry being killed in Whelan's was correct as he had heard it from Cashin. He would not part with any further information at the time but asked Hanley to wait for another week or so.

Frawley's movements were closely watched after that and he was seen to be often in Thomas Cashin's company.

On Tuesday 27 May Detective Hanley was speaking to ex-Garda Frawley's wife and she told him that at breakfast that morning her husband had said: 'There will be a nice laugh at the ... fellows who are looking for Larry if we get the body before them.' When she asked him what he meant by this he refused to enlighten her because he said that she would run to the barrack with the information. On 29 May 1930 ex-Garda Frawley and Thomas Cashin were observed surveying the Glen Bog while Paddy Whelan rested on the roadside nearby.

All of this led Hunt to believe that those involved in Larry Griffin's death were considering removing his body from its present position and placing it in the bog, where it would be 'found' by Cashin, Frawley and Whelan. On 29 May 1930 he wrote:

> For the past week or so I have been asked by different persons as to the position of the dismissed gardaí and Cashin in the event of the body being found in the bog and no evidence of foul play being discovered. One of the persons who approached me on this matter had admitted that it was on Whelan's instructions they were acting when they put me the question. I have good reason to believe the others were also acting on behalf of some of the other suspects. All this leads me to think there is a possibility of an early development and it may be that Frawley and Cashin were only selecting a suitable place in the bog for to find Griffin's body. The movements of all concerned are being closely watched night and day.

On Wednesday 4 June 1930, the *Munster Express* reported that over twenty villagers from Stradbally began another search of the Glen Bog in exceptionally fine weather conditions. The paper reported that the party included a number of those who had been accused of Griffin's murder. Although no names were mentioned it is safe to assume that the party included at the very least Thomas Cashin and Patrick Whelan, considering their recent surveying of the bog. It is not clear if ex-Garda Frawley participated in the search. The search party was equipped with pitchforks, iron hooks and other probing instruments. Large wooden planks were used to bridge over bog-holes which were being dragged. The paper reported that the 'villagers assert it is their intention to pursue the investigation until the entire area of bog is combed out'. The gardaí observed the activities with suspicion, wondering whether it was just for show or whether it was somehow intended to 'find' the body of Larry Griffin.

Meanwhile, Superintendent Hunt reported that Thomas Cashin had been visiting some old political friends near Carrick-on-Suir and that, in the course of a conversation about Larry Griffin, Cashin had told them that 'he would have told all long ago but for trying to save the Guards'. On 7 May armed detectives raided Cashin's house, presumably on the orders of Superintendent Hunt. They confiscated what was described as a sporting rifle and an amount of ammunition. According to the *Munster Express*, the raid was conducted so quietly that residents in the village were unaware of what was occurring. However, it seems that the confiscated items did not have any significance in terms of the investigation, and the raid may have been more for the purposes of harassing Cashin, in a situation where the gardaí clearly believed him to be a guilty party and were unable to get at him in any other way.

Hunt was also keeping a close eye on an eighteen-year-old man, Jim Murphy, an assistant gardener at the Woodhouse estate near Stradbally village. Murphy was one of the men who had been hanging about at Whelan's corner on Christmas evening, and he had been named by James Fitzgerald in his statement as one of the party who had entered Whelan's pub with him by the back door. However, like the other men named in Fitzgerald's statement, Murphy had denied this and by now, in any case, Fitzgerald had admitted that much of his statement was not true. Jim Murphy had been questioned several times in the early stages of the investigation, but had had nothing to say other than that he was outside Whelan's on Christmas evening and that he had seen the postman and Garda Dullea going around the corner.

Hunt described Jim Murphy as being 'of a quarrelsome disposition' and wrote that before Christmas Day 1929 'he was not regarded by members of the Whelan family as being anywhere near their social level'. However, according to Hunt, after the disappearance of Griffin a noticeable change occurred and 'it was observed that he was met with much more respect' whenever he called to Whelan's. After the release from prison of the Whelans and the other suspects, Murphy and his sister were invited to a social gathering of the Whelans' relations and friends in the public house. According to Hunt, 'this caused considerable comment locally and suggestions were made that Murphy knew something which Whelan desired to cloak'.

At the beginning of May, Murphy became involved in a fight with ex-Garda Frawley outside Whelan's pub. It was reported that during the row which led to the fight Murphy had said to Frawley that, if he was to 'take the lid off the pot' (presumably meaning if he were to tell all he knew), Frawley would regret Christmas night. It was also reported that the publican Patrick Whelan had tried to intervene to calm things down, but that the hot-headed Murphy had taken offence, believing that Whelan was taking sides against him. Murphy abused Frawley 'in the most vile language' and the two men came to blows. Sergeant O'Connor of Stradbally barracks and another garda had to intervene to separate the two men and to keep the peace. As Murphy was being held back by Sergeant O'Connor he was very agitated and he shouted at Frawley: 'If ye did your duty Frawley, like these men we have here now are doing it, Larry Griffin would be alive today.' Frawley kept his cool all the time but he seemed anxious for Murphy not to say any more in the presence of the gardaí. He was continually asking Murphy to move up the road with him so that they could settle their dispute without any outside interference. After this incident, Murphy struck up a friendship with Sergeant O'Connor. Superintendent Hunt was convinced that Murphy knew a great deal more about what had happened on Christmas night and, with Sergeant O'Connor's help, he hoped in due course to persuade him to tell all.

Around 22 May Superintendent Hunt reported that he had had a lengthy interview with Jim Murphy:

He was very frank in giving his opinions but when pressed for facts he was evasive. He is I think afraid of getting into trouble because he made the following remark to the sergeant two or three days ago – 'If I admitted to them when they questioned me that I was in Whelan's I would surely be arrested and sent to Waterford gaol.'

Superintendent Hunt wrote that the circumstances under which he had interviewed Murphy were not favourable for getting him to talk frankly. Hunt intended to provide a more favourable opportunity in the course of the next few days.

In a subsequent interview which Superintendent Hunt had with Murphy late one night at Tramore garda station, the latter said that he had actually seen Garda Dullea and Larry Griffin enter Whelan's back yard on Christmas night, and he claimed that the body of Larry Griffin was buried in the grounds of the Woodhouse estate. Hunt pressed him as to his reason for stating this:

he said that some days after the Guards were transferred from Stradbally he noticed a freshly made grave in a secluded part of the Demesne. When asked if he would point out the spot he appeared somewhat reluctant but eventually agreed to meet Detective Officer Hanley next day at 12 noon and show him the spot.

It was almost 3 a.m. in the morning when Superintendent Hunt and Detective Officer Hanley got back to Stradbally with Murphy after the interview; when they reached his house, Murphy's sister and mother were waiting up for him and according to Hunt 'both abused him for being out so late and for being in the company of the guards'. Detective Officer Hanley kept the appointment at 12 noon the next day but Murphy did not turn up. Hanley did meet him in the demesne later that day but Murphy then said he knew nothing about where Larry was buried. However, on being pressed he took Hanley to a mound of earth which looked like a grave and having pointed it out he ran away. When Hanley opened the grave he found it contained the body of a dead cow.

Repeated efforts were made after this to get Murphy into conversation about Griffin's disappearance, but to no avail, and Superintendent Hunt believed that this was due to the influence of his mother and sister:

> from the manner in which he declared the body was buried in the demesne I had every reason to believe he was speaking with some knowledge. His sister is a virago of the worst type and it is well known she exercises a considerable influence over him and were it not for this I do believe we might have got some useful information from him as to the final disposal of Griffin's body.

Chapter 19

Six months after the disappearance of Larry Griffin, the Bishop of Waterford and Lismore, Dr Hackett, finally intervened publicly in the missing postman case. The bishop had been aware for a long time that many practising Catholics in Stradbally were complicit in the death of Larry Griffin and in the denial of a Christian burial to the postman. He had also rebuffed General O'Duffy's earlier request for him to speak out. His intervention, though late, was far from half-hearted. Speaking with deep emotion at the parish confirmation service in Ballylaneen church in June 1930, the bishop denied suggestions that he had come to denounce the people, but said that he was pained by what had happened in the parish: 'Meeting my fellow bishops I have to hang my head in shame. The Stradbally "mystery" is spoken of in far-off Australia. Why "mystery"? There should be no mystery about it.' Then in a thinly veiled attack on the Whelans he continued:

I have information that should satisfy any man of intelligence that drink was distributed freely in Stradbally on Christmas Day last

> and also on Christmas Night. At what house or by whom I will
> not say. Such a shameful celebration of Christmas I denounce. It
> is disgraceful and unworthy of any Catholic community.

Dr Hackett added that for some time he had seriously considered the question of not visiting the parish until the affair was cleared up and the stain removed, but for the sake of the little children, and the local priest Father O'Shea, he had waived the intention of abstention. He appealed to the congregation to help clear up the matter and remove the cloud hanging over the district. 'Is it possible,' he asked, 'that if the postman is alive or dead that nobody knows anything about him?' The bishop prayed that Almighty God would throw light on the awful affair. The full force of ecclesiastical authority was now taking a firm stand alongside the state and against those in the community who had been complicit in the postman's death and disappearance.

However, even the bishop's strongly worded intervention did not bring about a breakthrough. The gardaí were no closer to solving the case. Just like Chief Superintendent O'Mara before him, as the failure of his investigations became more apparent, Superintendent Hunt became tardier in keeping HQ informed of developments. During his final three weeks in Stradbally, Hunt sent no report to HQ, and he returned to his own division in Galway on 21 June without furnishing a final report. Despite several requests from Deputy Commissioner

Coogan, it was not until 13 January 1931 that Hunt sent his final report on the Stradbally investigation.

In this last report, Superintendent Hunt strongly promoted the theory that Jim Murphy of Woodhouse knew more than he had told, and that he was a man 'to keep in touch with' for the purposes of getting to the bottom of the mystery. It may be, however, that Superintendent Hunt attached too much importance to Jim Murphy. Hunt had been parachuted in by HQ to replace O'Mara as head of the investigation and there had been high hopes that he was going to solve the mystery. Like O'Mara before him, therefore, Hunt was under a lot of pressure to be able to show that he had at least come up with productive new lines of enquiry. But by the time he left Stradbally and returned to Galway, all his enquiries had in effect come to nothing. This may have led him to exaggerate the extent to which Jim Murphy had provided new information after the fight with Frawley outside Whelan's pub.

Hunt claimed that, the first time he questioned him, Jim Murphy denied being anywhere in the vicinity of Whelan's pub on Christmas night, but that in subsequent interviews he admitted being at Whelan's corner that night and seeing Dullea and Griffin go around the corner and enter Whelan's back yard. In fact, the investigation files showed that Jim Murphy had given an account of being at Whelan's corner and of seeing Dullea and Larry Griffin go round the corner in his very first witness statement, given before Superintendent Hunt had even arrived in Stradbally. The only difference between Murphy's first statement and Hunt's account of his new evidence is that, according to Hunt, Murphy said he actually saw Dullea and Griffin go into the back yard, whereas in his witness statement he only says he saw them go around the corner. But this could have been another exaggeration on the part of Hunt. Murphy's talk during the fight outside Whelan's about 'lifting the lid' could have been no more than bravado, for, as Hunt himself admits, Murphy was a quick-tempered character and after the fight he clearly held a grudge against Garda Frawley. Murphy's claim about the body being buried in the Woodhouse estate yielded nothing except the bizarre incident involving the dead cow. In short, there is nothing to suggest that Murphy gave any significant new evidence after the fight outside Whelan's pub or as a result of Superintendent Hunt's interviews with him.

There was, however, possibly one useful piece of information which Hunt gleaned from Jim Murphy. This did not involve Murphy changing any part of his previous evidence. It was rather a case of Hunt picking up on something that had previously been ignored, because it had not fitted in with Jim Fitzgerald's witness statement, which the gardaí had at first accepted at face value. Murphy told Superintendent Hunt that Ned Morrissey was not in the vicinity of Whelan's pub on Christmas night. Apart from Jim Fitzgerald, no other witness had ever stated that they saw Ned Morrissey anywhere near Whelan's pub that night. In fact, Larry O'Brien, one of the men who had been outside Whelan's pub for some of the night, stated that he called into Morrissey's house at about 8.30 p.m. or 9 p.m. and that Morrissey was then sitting at the fire with his boots off. Jim Murphy, Larry O'Brien and John Power all admitted seeing the schoolteacher Cashin getting drink at Whelan's hall door at about 7.30 p.m. and then going back to his own house. Superintendent Hunt believed that Cashin must have returned to Whelan's later and entered by the back door. However, he now came to the conclusion that Morrissey was not in Whelan's pub at all on Christmas night and he did not believe that a man of Morrissey's 'character and standing' would have been allowed into the secret afterwards by Patrick Whelan, Thomas Cashin or Gardaí Dullea and Murphy. Hunt questioned Morrissey minutely regarding his movements on Christmas Day and night and Morrissey 'was not the least hesitant in answering my questions and his attitude generally left the impression that he was guiltless'. Hunt formed a very different impression of Cashin:

> I have no doubt whatever but he knows all about the death and what brought it about and unless I am greatly mistaken he is wholly responsible for it. In the disposal of the body he had the assistance of Dullea, [Garda] Murphy and Paddy Whelan, but outside these and perhaps Frawley and some members of Whelan's family I do not believe there is more information to be got.

Superintendent Hunt was also inclined to give some credence to the suggestions that Larry Griffin's death occurred in the garda barracks, although there was nothing to substantiate this theory other than rumours. Even if the postman had died in the barracks, however, Hunt was convinced that he had at the very least been injured in Whelan's pub before being brought to the barracks for the following reason:

> When Mrs Whelan was questioned about putting a blanket around Larry she denied it but stated that the blanket was put around an old man … who fell ill in the kitchen on some date around Christmas. The old man in question emphatically denied this when questioned and signed a written statement to this effect. His statement was borne out by others and there is no doubt but Mrs Whelan told a falsehood when she stated the blanket was brought to the kitchen for him. It is difficult to understand her reason for this falsehood unless when confronted with the assertion that a blanket was brought to the kitchen for Larry she was unable to give a blank denial and merely sidestepped the point by explaining it was required for a different man.

Hunt ended his final report on the case of the missing postman with his own personal theory on what had transpired – that it was the school principal Thomas Cashin who had the row with the postman, that it was Cashin who knocked Griffin down, that it occurred in Whelan's pub and that Griffin, while still unconscious, was taken across to the barracks where he died. Apart from Thomas Cashin, ex-Gardaí Murphy and Dullea and some members of the Whelan family, Hunt did not believe that anyone else knew the real facts. He also believed that Patrick Whelan the publican was not present when the row happened: 'He was, as far as I could ascertain, stupidly drunk from about 9 p.m. and incapable of understanding anything that occurred. Naturally enough he has been made conversant with the details since, particularly anything his wife knows.' Superintendent Hunt had come to Stradbally with a great belief in his own abilities and with strong faith placed in him by the garda commissioner. He had held out the prospect of a breakthrough in the case on several occasions. In the end, however, the silent village did not let him in on its secret.

Chapter 20

When Thomas Cashin was charged with murder in January 1930, he was suspended without pay from his position as principal of Ballylaneen National School and replaced by a temporary teacher, Cornelius Wall. However, Mrs Cashin continued in her position as second teacher in the school. When the case against Cashin and the others collapsed in March, Cashin expected to be reinstated in his former position as a matter of course – he was after all innocent in the eyes of the law. But the records show that the authorities were extremely reluctant to allow him back. Over a period of months after the dismissal of the case, both Cashin and his solicitor Peter O'Connor were writing to the Department of Education seeking his reinstatement. At the same time there were discussions and correspondence about the matter between the Department of Education, the Department of Justice and An Garda Síochána.

The Department of Education proposed to hold an enquiry into Cashin's behaviour in relation to the Larry Griffin case, and on 28 March 1930 the secretary of the Department of Education, P. Ó Brolacháin, wrote to Cashin, asking him to respond to the allegations made against him that he had been present in a pub on Christmas Day, that he had been involved in the killing or wounding of Larry Griffin, and that his motor car had been used for the removal of the body. Ó Brolacháin stated that there was:

> the further question as to whether you have given to the Authorities of the State such assistance as it is in your power to give in order to enable them to clear up this very serious case and to fix the responsibility for what occurred.

Far from welcoming Cashin back into the fold as a person who had been unjustly accused and subsequently vindicated, the department was refusing to accept the decision of the court on the matter as final and was, in effect, conducting a quasi-judicial review of the case. Their attitude to Cashin must have been coloured, in part, by his troublesome disposition and poor performance as a teacher in the years before the missing postman case.

Because the gardaí never took a formal statement from Thomas Cashin, it is only in his correspondence with the Department of Education that we finally hear his defence of himself in relation to the disappearance of Larry Griffin. On 3 April he responded to the department denying all the allegations made against him. He said he considered it very unjust that he had to suffer further as a result of a statement 'made by a man named Fitzgerald known to all as the oddest and most eccentric man in the village'. He pointed out that Fitzgerald had subsequently recanted his statement in court. He claimed that Fitzgerald had said that his statement had all been 'forced out of him' – a rather selective use of Fitzgerald's contradictory and incoherent evidence while on the stand. Cashin stated that his solicitor had informed him 'that the State authorities are at least satisfied that Fitzgerald's story was an invention, and that no alleged murder or assault of Griffin took place in Whelans, or that his body was removed in a motor car'. At best this was wishful thinking on Cashin's part – at worst a deliberate attempt to mislead the department. Cashin claimed that no man was more astounded than he was after Christmas when news reached Stradbally that Larry Griffin was missing, and he pointed out that he had immediately offered his motor car to convey the gardaí all over the countryside in search of Griffin. He said that he:

> discussed the matter with the guards and the people of the village
> and was always at the disposal of the superintendents, detectives
> and guards to help in every way to clear up the mystery and give
> all possible information at my disposal.

He argued that he had been most unjustly put under suspicion simply because he happened to be the owner of the only motor car in the village. He also wrote that he never had any dispute with or ill will towards Larry Griffin, 'but on the contrary I liked the man and would not deliberately do him an injury or permit any other person to do so in my presence'. Finally he wrote:

> I strongly resent the reflection on my character as a good Irishman and Catholic that I would violently assault or murder another human being or that if I saw any man seriously injured or dying that I would not rush for priest, doctor and police authorities. I have been acquitted of the foul charge brought against me by a disreputable labourer of low character and antecedents. To clear myself and my children hereafter I court the fullest inquiry to prove conclusively my innocence. May I therefore respectfully request that the proposed inquiry by your Board should be held without further delay.

Superintendent Hunt, who was then still in Stradbally, was asked to comment on Cashin's letter for the benefit of the Department of Education. In his report of 20 May 1930, Hunt claimed that:

> 99% of the public in this area have no hesitation in stating he [Cashin] is one of the guilty parties. Apart from his own near relatives and the immediate relatives of those who were charged with him no one speaks to him and his social position since his release from prison is most unenviable. It has been noticed that

in bars of licensed premises most of his former associates turn
their backs on him, or leave when he enters, rather than be seen
in his company.

It does appear to be the case that the vast majority of people in
Stradbally believed Cashin to have been associated with Larry
Griffin's death, and there was certainly a significant amount of
hostility to those believed to have been involved. However, I
believe that Superintendent Hunt exaggerated the extent to
which Cashin was ostracised. In a small village like Stradbally,
the relatives and friends of the ten accused persons accounted
for a sizeable proportion of the population. In general, Cashin
and the other accused were some of the most influential people
in the area, and it is clear from press reports that they had a
significant number of supporters during the court case.

Superintendent Hunt also wrote that it was 'well known
to quite a number of people' that Cashin had been in Griffin's
company in Whelan's on Christmas night, and that it was
also well known that it was Cashin and not the labourer Ned
Morrissey who had inflicted the injuries which had resulted
in Griffin's death. However, Hunt stated that nothing would
induce those people who could give evidence to come forward
and state the facts. He attributed this 'to apathy on the part
of a large section of the public and to intimidation exercised
by the accused and their friends on the remainder'. The
superintendent wrote that, apart from the parties that were

accused, no acquaintance of Jim Fitzgerald would describe him as the 'oddest and most eccentric man in the village', and stated that Fitzgerald had a very good reputation in the area.

While agreeing that Cashin had utilised his motor car in the search for Griffin, Hunt pointed out that the only members of the garda conveyed by him were those as deeply implicated in Griffin's disappearance as himself:

> It is true that for several days following Christmas day he took either Guards Dullea or Murphy, two of the men who were later charged with the crime, or Guard Frawley, who is also suspected, around in his car in a pretended search for Griffin.

However, Hunt went even further, claiming that this search 'consisted merely of calling to the various public-houses in the surrounding districts and spending most of the time drinking stout at the bar'. Whether or not this is another exaggeration on Hunt's part, it is hard to disagree with his conclusion that the whole aim of this 'display of anxiety' on Cashin's part 'was only to throw dust in the eyes of the people'.

Hunt reported that, in a conversation with Garda Peter Twamley in Waterford on 3 January 1930, Cashin had said that 'he would make a liar of anyone who would say that Larry Griffin or Guard Dullea were seen going around Whelan's corner together, that he [Cashin] and Dullea had it arranged to say they spent the day together in Ballylaneen'. Furthermore,

Garda Twamley had reported another conversation on 16 January during which he had asked Cashin if he had yet been approached for a statement about Griffin's disappearance. Cashin had replied that he had not been approached and that he intended to see Garda Murphy before he made any statement. The only deduction to be drawn from this, according to Hunt, was that Cashin intended to arrange beforehand with Garda Murphy what he was to say in the event of being interviewed. Cashin also said to Garda Twamley that he had met Garda Dullea in the village on Christmas night at ten o'clock but he asked Twamley 'for God's sake to say nothing about it as they all had jobs to lose'. The garda files confirm that Garda Peter Twamley did indeed report these two conversations with Thomas Cashin as Hunt outlined them. In view of these conversations with Garda Twamley, Hunt argued that Cashin's 'protests about not being interviewed and his statement that he was willing and anxious to help in every way may be regarded as more "bluff" on his part'.

Hunt himself had finally interviewed Cashin on 10 May, and was fully convinced of his guilt:

> He showed no desire whatever to help and although he vehemently denied being in Whelan's on Christmas night, or seeing Larry Griffin after about 2.30 p.m., his answers to all my questions were evasive and unconvincing. He denied being at or near Whelan's Licensed premises at any time during the evening or

night of Christmas Day, but there is ample proof that between 6.30 p.m. and 7.00 p.m. on that night he was outside Whelan's front door and got a bottle of stout through the door from Whelan's son Philip, a schoolboy eleven years old.

The garda files corroborate Hunt on this point. Both Jim Murphy of Woodhouse and John Power of Carrigahilla had seen Cashin get the drink at Whelan's front door.

Hunt said that when questioned by him about the statement he had made to Garda Peter Twamley, Cashin had denied the remarks and called Garda Twamley a liar. When pressed for a theory as to what had become of Griffin he could offer none and 'generally his attitude was that of a guilty man who holds that a person is presumed innocent until the contrary is proved'.

Hunt finished his report with a strongly worded argument against Cashin being allowed to resume his position at Ballylaneen National School:

Every intelligent man or woman I have spoken to about Cashin are agreed that he is guilty to some degree in Griffin's disappearance and generally the public are alarmed lest he might be re-instated in his position as school teacher. I believe such a course would create a very bad feeling in the public mind. Apart from himself and his wife I do not think there is another person in the locality has any desire to see him re-instated in his former position. As Principal of Ballylaneen School he could never hope to maintain any sort of discipline as the schoolchildren, as well as their parents, believe absolutely in his guilt. When he was in prison his wife, who is teaching with him, had occasion to punish two children in the school one day and on the following day the mother of the children came to the school and told Mrs Cashin to go and hand over Larry Griffin's body before she would again punish her children. This is the attitude I fear would be adopted towards Cashin if he is allowed to return to his school.

Meanwhile the Department of Education had written again to Cashin asking him to clarify some matters, and to give an account of his movements on Christmas Day. Cashin responded giving a very detailed account of his movements which closely matched the statement his wife had given during the garda investigation, and which did not involve being in Whelan's pub at any time. He made no mention of obtaining drink at Whelan's front door early on Christmas night, as he had been observed doing by several witnesses. He argued forcefully that he had been:

> cruelly treated, maligned and unjustly suspected through the hostility and blunders of the superior officers of the Garda Síochána, one of whom said when charging me after I was arrested, 'I knew from the first that you were the murderer of Larry Griffin'.

In a passage which gives an indication of the close relationship between Cashin and the likes of Gardaí Dullea and Murphy, Cashin said that one of the reasons he had come under suspicion was 'because some of the guards in Stradbally used visit my house when off duty to hear my wireless set and to go shooting with me, as I kept a gun and good dogs'.

In spite of Cashin's spirited defence of himself, the Department of Education continued to write to him pressing him for more information and clarification. At this stage Cashin had not only been suspended, but had also been deprived of his salary for seven months, and his frustration was beginning to show. In the course of a lengthy and emotively worded letter to the department on 21 July, Cashin once again cast himself in the role of persecuted victim:

The people of the village and surrounding districts have confidence in me and know that from my past antecedents and character, I would not be the inhuman monster, the brutal savage that Fitzgerald alleged assisted in killing a simple, unoffending man (whom I and everybody liked), that before he was actually dead and without sending for a priest or doctor, Mrs Whelan (admitted to be the most pious woman in Stradbally and who received Holy Communion on this Christmas morning) sewed his body up in a blanket with a 56 lbs. weight attached, and that I then took the dying or dead man in my motor car to a mine hole, and without Christian burial flung him down on top of the putrid carcasses of animals. Such a story on the face of it was so unreal, so impossible in Catholic Ireland, and alleged to have happened on the great Festival Day of Christmas was a scandalous reflection, not alone on the ten persons arrested, but on the whole Irish race. Because the authorities made a blunder in arresting ten innocent persons on Fitzgerald's false and uncorroborated statement and before the body of the postman was found, the press of the world for financial gain published lurid stories and pictures from day to day for a period of nearly three months about this strange case, injuring our credit and reputation.

By now the Department of Education had finally begun to accept that any enquiry they could hold was unlikely to uncover new evidence which neither the courts nor An Garda Síochána had discovered. However, they still procrastinated, hoping that the case against Cashin might be reopened and legal proceedings renewed. Then in October they tried to pass the responsibility for making a decision on Cashin's future to the bishop of Waterford and Lismore. According to a departmental memorandum they wrote to Bishop Hackett stating that:

in all the circumstances it was considered that the question of Mr Cashin's resumption of duty was one which should be viewed primarily in regard to its local aspect, and that it was of such a nature as to lend itself to be more suitably dealt with by the manager in consultation with His Lordship.

Having consulted with the parish priest Fr Lannon, who was also the manager of the school, Bishop Hackett indicated that he felt that Cashin should be reinstated. However, he acknowledged that some people in the parish were of the opinion that Cashin 'should not be allowed to continue as teacher'. This would seem to indicate that there was some truth to Superintendent Hunt's statements about the attitude of the community towards Cashin, even if he had overstated the case. Thomas Cashin was finally reinstated as principal of Ballylaneen National School on 18 December 1930.

That was not the end of the matter, however, for Cashin now sought back payment of his salary for the period during which he had not been allowed to teach. He had, after all, been suspended because of charges of which he had been cleared by the courts, but he had still lost almost a year's salary. The Irish National Teachers' Organisation made representations on his behalf, and after some consideration the Department of Education saw the logic of his argument, but convincing the Department of Finance to pay up was a different matter. In July 1931 the Cumann na nGaedheal Minister for Finance Ernest Blythe gave a direction that no payment be sanctioned for any part of the period during which Mr Cashin was under suspension and rendered no service to the school. However, the general election of 1932 brought Fianna Fáil to power, with the open support of the IRA. It seems the new administration looked more favourably on Cashin's case, perhaps because of his republican credentials – the new Minister for Education Seán MacEntee sanctioned the back payment of salary to Cashin.

Chapter 21

⸺◆⸺

'Another ten minutes and we'll have this field finished!'

Twenty-year-old Mike Murphy wiped the sweat from his forehead and grinned back at the speaker, his brother Danny. The two young men were saving the hay on a small farm in the Ring Gaeltacht and were speaking in their native Irish.

'Sure we'd have it finished long ago if it weren't for all your gabbering!'

Danny was about to fling a tuft of hay at his older brother in playful retaliation, but just then he saw their father Jamsie coming towards them across the small field. As well as owning a small farm, seventy-one-year-old Jamsie Murphy was the local postmaster and retired schoolmaster.

'Hey lads,' he called out to them, 'they're looking for a postman in Kilmacthomas.' Mike and Danny started laughing, thinking their father was talking about the search for the missing postman.

'Sure they've been looking for him for a year now!'

'Oh no,' said Jamsie, 'they're looking for someone to go down to Kilmacthomas to do the job for them.'

That was how Larry Griffin's replacement came to hear about the vacancy. Mike Murphy applied and was accepted for the job and worked the Stradbally route for twenty-five years. When he was moved from that route in 1955, he was presented with a clock and a gift of money in the parlour of Whelan's public house by Norah, the wife of James Whelan who had by then inherited the family business. A photograph published in one of the local newspapers on that occasion shows the postman arm in arm with James, one of those who had been arrested and charged with the murder of his predecessor. According to Mike Murphy's son Seán, who still lives in Kilmacthomas, when his father started working the Stradbally route he was given a garda escort every day from the Five Crossroads into Stradbally, and from Stradbally back out to the Five Crossroads, for fear he would come to any harm like his predecessor. This arrangement lasted until the beginning of the Second World War.

It is clear from the garda files that the Stradbally case remained 'a lasting disgrace to the garda', as Deputy Commissioner Coogan described it. Coogan felt that the case could not be allowed to rest, at least until Griffin's remains had been located, and he continued to exhort the local officers to pursue the investigation. On 7 January 1931, he wrote to Harry O'Mara's replacement in Waterford, Chief Superintendent Leahy, suggesting that:

> now that the widespread publicity which the mystery of the postman's disappearance at first attracted has subsided local

people may be more willing to talk and discreet inquiries, if now renewed in a quiet way by the local garda, may lead to something useful being ascertained.

Again on 23 July 1931, Coogan wrote to the chief superintendent that 'the time is now opportune for a determined effort, under your personal direction, to bring this case to a successful conclusion'. There are many pages of unsigned handwritten notes in the garda files which show that the local garda party did keep their eyes and ears open in an attempt to gather useful intelligence which might lead to a breakthrough in the case.

The Whelan family encountered a certain amount of hostility in the locality in the aftermath of the missing postman case and there must have been some fall-off in business as a result of this. Considering the precarious position of Patrick Whelan's financial affairs before Christmas 1929, this might have been expected to finally put him out of business. However, the missing postman case proved to be the Whelans' financial salvation in the form of libel damages. In July 1930 the family between them won the colossal sum of £1,740 damages against Waterford News Ltd, publishers of the *Evening News*. The damages related to the ill-advised article which had appeared in that paper on 6 February 1930, after the arrests of members of the Whelan family but before the case against them had been outlined in court (see Chapter 11). The article had recounted the version of Larry Griffin's death which was widely believed in the district and which was similar to Jim Fitzgerald's statement – that Larry Griffin had died after a scuffle in Whelan's pub and that his body had been disposed of. The article clearly implicated the Whelan family in the cover-up of a crime; however, with the collapse of the state's case against them, they were innocent in the eyes of the law, which left the *Evening News* badly exposed over what they had published. The Whelans' solicitor from the criminal case, Peter O'Connor, once more acted on their behalf in the libel action. The Whelans later won damages for a similar article which had been published in the *Cork Examiner* around the same time.

Patrick Whelan's portion of the *Evening News* damages – £700 – was immediately seized through the courts by one of his creditors. Due to her youth, Cissie's portion of the damages was to be kept in trust for her, but she was able to use the award as security to help raise a loan of £90 to help her father pay off some more of his debts. As it happened, the loan came from Thomas Cashin, who was by then again enjoying the security of his regular salary. Presumably the rest of the Whelan family's damages also helped pay off other creditors.

Even this was not enough to clear all the debts, however, and in October 1931 Lady Emily Frances Hodson of the Woodhouse estate obtained an ejection decree against Whelan for non-payment of rent for the public house and hotel. The arrears amounted to £16 11s and 8d. But Whelan was not subsequently ejected from the premises, so it seems that he managed to pay off his arrears, probably with the damages from the *Cork Examiner* case. Taking into account Patrick Whelan's dire financial situation at the time of Larry Griffin's disappearance, and the amount of libel damages won by the family, it is hardly going too far to say that the missing postman case saved Patrick Whelan's business from bankruptcy.

On 12 March 1931 the missing postman case was raised in Dáil Éireann by two Waterford TDs, Patrick Little of Fianna Fáil and Captain Willie Redmond, now an independent TD after the recent dissolution of his Irish National League Party. In his capacity as a barrister, Redmond had also represented some of the defendants in the case in court. The Minister for Justice, James Fitzgerald-Kenny, stated that he had personally read the statements of the entire Stradbally garda party. This indicated that the Stradbally case was causing concern at the highest levels of government. Patrick Little asked the minister whether he was 'aware that there is grave public dissatisfaction with the manner in which investigations were conducted by the garda into the case of Laurence Griffin'. He asked whether, in view of the unsatisfactory results of the garda investigation, the minister would agree to set up a tribunal of enquiry into the missing postman case.

In his reply, Minister Fitzgerald-Kenny acknowledged that the conduct of the police investigation had been marked by two regrettable incidents. These were, firstly, 'the failure of the gardaí who were stationed in Stradbally at the time of

Griffin's disappearance to report the matter at once and to give all possible assistance', and, secondly, 'the over-zeal of some of the members of the gardaí who were subsequently called in to assist in the investigation'. The minister said that the necessary disciplinary action had been taken in both cases. With these exceptions he felt that 'the investigation has been pursued over a long period with great energy' and he was 'confident that the public realise that the lack of success up to the present is not due to any fault on the part of the gardaí'. He refused the request to set up a tribunal of enquiry into the case:

> I do not see what useful purpose could be served by any such tribunal unless it were armed with powers more extensive than it has been thought proper to entrust even to the highest courts under our present judicial system, including the power to compel witnesses to give answers incriminating themselves.

However, Mr Little continued to press the minister on the matter:

Mr Little: Is the Minister satisfied with the conduct of the Guards in the investigation of this case?

Mr Fitzgerald-Kenny: I think in the beginning matters were carried out very badly but I think afterwards they were carried out with great zeal and skill.

Mr Little: Is the Minister satisfied with the slow progress being made now?

Mr Fitzgerald-Kenny: I am satisfied the Guards are doing all
that it is possible to do. If the people in the neighbourhood
will not come forward and give information they ought to
give, the Guards are, of course, much hampered.

Mr Little: Is the Minister aware that there is a whole parish
under the unproved charge of murder?

Mr Fitzgerald-Kenny: No, I am not.

Mr Little: That is the public feeling.

The attitude of the Minister for Justice to the Stradbally case
must have been influenced to some degree by the ferocious
conflict between the IRA and the state, a conflict which had
intensified in the latter years of the Cumann na nGaedheal
administration. The gardaí were in the front line of this fight,
and many members of the force had been brutally killed by
the 'irregulars' (IRA) in their campaign to undermine the state.
Furthermore, the minister would have been aware that the
sympathies of many people in the Stradbally area would not
have been entirely on the side of the state in this conflict. There
was a strong republican tradition in the district, and the IRA
itself was active in the area. This could have been another factor
inhibiting the flow of information to the gardaí about the case.

In early September 1931, the gardaí received information
that an IRA meeting had been held at Woodhouse, Stradbally,
about 4 a.m. on the morning of 23 August and that it had
been attended by, among others, Thomas Cashin, the school

principal, and James Whelan, the son of the publican. As a result of this information, Cashin, Whelan and others who were believed to have attended the meeting were kept under observation, but the gardaí did not have enough powers to take any action against them at that point. This was soon to change, for in October the government brought in a new piece of legislation to help counter the IRA threat – the Constitution (Amendment No. 17) Act. The new legislation gave the gardaí new and wide-ranging powers. 'The basic idea,' as Conor Brady writes, 'was to make life hell for the rank and file supporter of violent Republicanism.'[2] The new act enabled the gardaí to do this without the fear of legal repercussions they had previously felt. Acting on these new powers, a senior officer from Tramore garda station, Superintendent Kelly, paid several visits to Thomas Cashin's house to question and warn him about his alleged IRA activities.

The first of Superintendent Kelly's visits took place on 14 November 1931, when he was accompanied by Garda Cunniffe of Stradbally station. According to Kelly's account Cashin was 'at first indignant about my calling'. Kelly questioned Cashin about his movements during the month of August, especially on the morning of 23 August. Cashin denied being involved in any way with IRA activities, and said he could not remember what he was doing on the dates mentioned by Kelly. According to Kelly, Cashin 'became more amicable before I left, and said

---

2   Conor Brady (1974), p. 159

he would look up the dates, and that he would satisfy me that he was not connected with any irregular organisation'. Kelly's second visit took place on 10 December 1931 and he was accompanied by Sergeant O'Connor of Stradbally. As well as questioning Cashin about his alleged IRA activities, Kelly also questioned him about the missing postman case.

The third visit took place on 30 December 1931 and on this occasion Kelly was unaccompanied 'as I thought he [Cashin] might be more disposed to talk to me without a third person present'. Kelly questioned Cashin about his association with another suspected member of the IRA, James Gough of Leamybrien, but Cashin said that he had only ever met Gough a few times and that he could not remember when he last met him. According to Kelly, Cashin's 'manner was shifty and uneasy, and it was obvious that he was not telling me the truth'. The missing postman case also came up in the course of this conversation. According to Kelly, Cashin 'appeared most anxious to impress me about his innocence in the matter'. Cashin said he strongly desired to have the matter cleared up 'as there would be a slur over himself and his family and on the village of Stradbally as long as it was unsolved'.

The conversation then took a bizarre turn. Superintendent Kelly brought up a rumour circulating in Stradbally, to the effect that the village was cursed as a result of the missing postman case. Two people had recently died at a young age. One of them, a Mrs Cleary, had been the barrack servant at

Stradbally when Larry Griffin disappeared and it was rumoured that her husband William Cleary had buried Griffin's body. The other person who died was Thomas Carthy, who was supposed to have been told about Griffin's death on Christmas night by one of those who had been present in the pub. As well as these deaths, both Ned Morrissey and one of the Whelan girls, either Cissie or Nora, had recently been taken seriously ill. The supposed curse was much talked about by the people of Stradbally and Kilmacthomas, and Superintendent Kelly mentioned it to Cashin to see its effect on him, as Cashin was 'naturally highly strung'. According to Kelly, Cashin 'got very excited and uneasy' when the curse was raised. 'He moved about in the chair, and clutched his trousers.'

Kelly suggested to Cashin that he was in Whelan's pub on Christmas night 1929 but Cashin insisted that he did not enter Whelan's at all that day. Cashin asked how it was that Sergeant Cullinane did not see him in Whelan's, seeing as the sergeant had visited the house twice that day. Kelly suggested that Sergeant Cullinane and Cashin were so friendly that the sergeant would avoid meeting Cashin. According to Kelly's report, Cashin admitted that this was true and that 'the sergeant would not catch him if he could avoid him'. Kelly suggested that Cashin had been in the snug in Whelan's but Cashin denied this. Kelly wrote in his report: 'I had heard that Cashin used to go into the snug when entering Whelan's after hours, and that he and Sergeant Cullinane had an arrangement to that effect.'

At the beginning of January 1932 the solicitor Peter O'Connor, acting on behalf of Cashin, wrote to Superintendent Kelly to complain about these visits. O'Connor alleged that Kelly had abused his powers 'in questioning Mr Cashin, making unfair allegations, demanding admission into his private residence and thereby indirectly frightening his wife and young children'. The letter ended with a threat of future legal action over what had occurred. According to Superintendent Kelly, the solicitor's description of his visits to Cashin was highly inaccurate. He said that the questions he asked Cashin were 'purely conversational' and that he did not insist on answers. Kelly denied that he had demanded admittance into Cashin's house and stated that on each of his visits he was invited by Cashin and his wife into the sitting-room.

Superintendent Kelly's superiors were not in the least bit worried by the solicitor's intervention. They believed that Superintendent Kelly had a perfect legal right to question Cashin and anybody else whom they thought could assist with their enquiries. Chief Superintendent Leahy in Waterford regarded O'Connor's threatening letter 'as mere bluff and a continuation of his efforts to intimidate in a quiet way the gardaí in this division from pursuing investigations into the Stradbally case'. The gardaí seem to have been correct in their belief that O'Connor was bluffing on his client's behalf, for nothing further seems to have come of the matter.

In April 1932, Patrick Whelan sent an extraordinary letter

to the Minister for Justice seeking permission to use explosives to search for the body of Larry Griffin. He referred in the letter to the serious illness of one of his daughters, and to recent continuing press reports about the missing postman case. These reports had given his sick daughter 'endless pain,' he wrote, and he himself had 'suffered enough mental and physical torture to undermine a man's reason'. He felt that he 'should take some drastic action to end an intolerable situation'. He was, he wrote, firmly convinced that 'poor Griffin' fell into the Glen Bog and that his body was still there. The only way to determine this would be 'to blow the water from the various bog-holes by means of explosives'. He asked for permission to purchase a sufficient amount of gelignite for this purpose. 'The finding of Griffin's body,' he wrote, 'would solve forever this so-called mystery and silence the malicious and lying tongues that find delight in the misfortunes of their neighbours.' His family's name would be 'cleared of an odious stigma finally' and he would 'know some mental peace'.

The Department of Justice sought the advice of An Garda Síochána in relation to Patrick Whelan's request. Chief Superintendent J. Murphy in Waterford was of the opinion that the granting of the authorisation requested by Whelan would not result in Griffin's body being discovered. The gardaí were still convinced that the body was not in the bog, which had been thoroughly searched following Griffin's disappearance. Chief Superintendent Murphy suggested that Whelan's motive in making the application was to show himself to the authorities in a favourable light: 'He wants to show his anxiety to have the body recovered and thereby clear himself from the stigma of having been concerned in Griffin's disappearance.' The gardaí were of the opinion that Whelan knew exactly where the body was, and that his application was not genuine. However, Chief Superintendent Murphy thought that, if the application was refused, Whelan would 'probably endeavour to show that in his efforts to locate Griffin's body he is being hindered by the Authorities'. In view of this, he recommended that the application be granted subject to the explosives being used under garda supervision. The Department of Justice accepted this advice and wrote to Whelan to tell him to apply to his local garda superintendent for a permit to purchase and use explosives. However, there is no evidence in the files to indicate that Whelan ever proceeded with his plan to purchase and use explosives to search the Glen Bog.

Meanwhile Larry Griffin's bicycle, which had been found on the bog road the morning after his disappearance, remained for a number of years in Stradbally garda barracks. In the absence of Larry's body, it was in a sense the most tangible reminder of the missing postman. Presumably, it was being held onto as potential evidence, but it must have been a stark reminder of the unsolved mystery that still cast a shadow over the village. In 1943 the postmaster in Kilmacthomas, Tom Brown, received instructions from his superiors in Waterford to retrieve the bicycle. Brown had one of his postmen, Seamus O'Brien, hire a donkey and cart to go to Stradbally and get the bicycle. The last remaining physical reminder of Larry Griffin's existence had gone from Stradbally.

Once O'Brien had brought the bicycle back to Kilmacthomas, it was sent on to Waterford. Considering that the post office thought it worth their while to recover the bicycle, it must have been pressed into service again in some other district, and another postman must have delivered his mail on Larry Griffin's bicycle, unaware of its tragic history.

Chapter 22

Over the years the case of the missing postman has continued to fascinate the Irish folk and literary imagination. Various stories about where Larry Griffin's body lies are to be heard not just in County Waterford but in many parts of Ireland. The origin of some of these stories can be traced back to the files of An Garda Síochána.

In September 1930, Garda Sergeant C. Horgan, who was based in Wexford, was on holiday at his home at Shanaway, Ballineen, County Cork. A sister of his, Bessie Horgan, told him that she had heard a strange grave had been made in Fanlobbus graveyard, Dunmanway, a short time after the previous Christmas. According to Sergeant Horgan, this 'newly made grave was apparently seen and no one could account for it being made there or know who was buried in it. It was spoken of as a strange thing.' Horgan returned to Wexford and forgot about the matter until December 1930, when it occurred to him that perhaps the strange grave had a connection with the missing postman case: 'The graveyard mentioned would be suitable to Ex-Guard Edward Dullea whom I suspect to have had a hand in the hiding of the body ... The home of ex-Garda E. Dullea is about three to four miles from the place.' However, after some investigation the gardaí came to the conclusion that the strange grave had been made for a stillborn child, which accounted for the secrecy surrounding it.

Early in 1934, a Garda Superintendent Bergin received information about a strange and grisly discovery that had been made at Castletownkenneigh graveyard in County Cork the previous year. On 8 November 1933, when the body of Michael Sullivan of Shancastle was being buried in the Sullivan plot in Castletownkenneigh graveyard, a partly decomposed human leg was found about one and a half feet below the surface. The last person buried in this grave had been a Cornelius Sullivan who had died in 1895, and whose remains should have been fully decomposed by 1933. The plot itself was very neglected as the deceased man, Michael Sullivan, was the last of the family and was described as being 'very poor'. One of the gravediggers on the day even remarked half in jest that the remains must have been those of the missing postman, Larry Griffin. They replaced the remains in the grave along with the coffin of Michael Sullivan. However, when Superintendent Bergin later heard of the strange occurrence, he took it quite seriously and statements were taken from the gravediggers. It was suggested that the remains may have belonged to one Cornelius Cronin of Shancastle whose leg had been amputated in the North Infirmary hospital in Cork in August 1932. However, it was established that Cronin's leg had been buried in a wooden box in the family's burial plot in Inchigeela, County Cork, and that it was still there in January 1933 when the grave was opened for the burial of another family member. Having reviewed the evidence, garda headquarters in Dublin decided that an exhumation order was not warranted as there would be no way of telling if the leg belonged to Larry Griffin. In the era before DNA techniques, the only way to identify such remains was through the observation of distinctive features. It was known, for example, that Larry Griffin had a war wound in his collar bone which had disabled his arm, and that some of his teeth were missing, but there was no known distinctive feature which could be used to identify his leg. Therefore 'the mystery of the Castletownkenneigh leg' remains unresolved to this day.

On the *CSÍ* programme in 2009, Larry Griffin's relatives made an appeal for anyone with information about the where-abouts of his body to come forward. As a result, a Leitrim man contacted them to tell a story which he had heard about the location of the body. The story, which he subsequently recounted for me, goes as follows:

About 1966 or 1967, when I was nineteen years of age, in a country pub that my father owned in Keadue, County Roscommon, the local sergeant was having a drink with my father in the snug late at night after the customers were gone. I was cleaning up glasses and they were talking about this story of Larry Griffin, the missing postman. The sergeant told my father that he [Larry Griffin] was buried behind the wall in Kilronan graveyard and that there was a barrel of tar on top of him. My father was asking the sergeant how he knew, and the sergeant said, 'It's on record in the barracks.'

There are also stories that Larry Griffin was buried somewhere in County Clare and Dr Tadhg Ó Dúshláine tells of a county councillor who 'knew for a fact' that the remains had been disposed of in Ravensdale forest in County Louth. Indeed Dr Ó Dúshláine has files full of folklore he has collected about the missing postman case.

The case of the missing postman has been a source of fascination for many creative writers, including Flann O'Brien. Though written in 1940, O'Brien's famous novel *The Third Policeman* was not published for another seventeen years. It opens with a shocking murder and most of the activities take place in a police station. Dr Tadhg Ó Dúshláine describes it as 'a satire on the violence, duplicity and incompetence of Irish society, inspired, in all probability by the case of the Missing Postman'.

Tadhg Ó Dúshláine has compiled the following list of other works which he believes may also have been inspired by the missing postman case:

Dead Star's Light by Elizabeth Connor (1938)

A novel set at Christmas 1919, against the background of the

War of Independence. As the story begins a crowd including the doctor, judge and bank manager are drinking in a pub after two o'clock in the morning. On the ten-mile drive home they kill a man and dispose of his body down a mineshaft. Though set before the events at Stradbally, the book was banned.

Leaves for Burning by Mervyn Wall (1952)

All the local dignitaries are on an illicit drinking spree for the weekend – the county manager, the schoolteacher, the local senator, the doctor. They are having a sing-song in the upper room of a local hostelry until a disgruntled labourer interrupts the session. They manhandle him, as a result of which he falls out the window and breaks his neck. 'Oh,' wails the publican, 'such a thing to have happened in my house.' They agree on a cover-up and the senator promises to have a word with the sergeant and coroner. This novel was also banned.

Prisoners of Silence by James Cheasty (1971)

A stage play based very closely on the case of the missing postman, which was first performed at the Gas Company Theatre, Dún Laoghaire, County Dublin, in April 1971 and later at Waterford's Theatre Royal. As a result of threats of libel actions it was not staged for many years but it was revived in 2009 by the Stagemad Theatre Company in Waterford.

Dark Rosaleen by Frank Delaney (1989)

A novel with direct similarities to the case of the missing postman. Various people are charged with the death of a postman, there is talk of the postman cracking his head on an iron stove and of his body being taken away in a car to be disposed of either down a mineshaft or where there are roadworks taking place.

Over the years journalists, like myself, have also been drawn back to the unsolved mystery, and many of the former defendants in the case developed a lucrative cottage industry taking libel actions against newspapers over articles relating to the case.

In July 1954 two of the former Stradbally garda party, William Murphy and John Sullivan, each claimed £600 libel damages against the publishers of a British newspaper, the *Empire News*, for an article which appeared under the name Beatrice Coogan. The offending passage read:

The village postman was plied with time-honoured hospitality and when he could hold no more upright he was taken to the police barracks for safety. They put him to bed – not in a chair, but comfortably in an upstairs room. During the night he left the room. There was no banister to the stairs. He stepped out into space and crashed to his death. None of this was generally known when the postman's bicycle was found in a bog by the road he would have taken home … White-faced witnesses were questioned over the shaft ... No one said a word, there was a wall of outraged silence that could never be broken ... nobody said a word and silence remained complete.

The case was settled in November 1954 and the ex-gardaí received an undisclosed amount in damages.

In 1961, four of the defendants in the missing postman case took an action against the British newspaper *The Sunday Telegraph*. The plaintiffs were James Whelan, Mrs Nora Orpen (née Whelan), George Cummins and Patrick Cunningham. The alleged libel was contained in an article under the heading 'Here in Youghal' by Claud Cockburn, the relevant portion of which was read out in court:

I gropingly feel there is some significance in a scene I witnessed the other day at a beach lunch-picnic organised for a lot of children on a strand between here and Waterford.

All sorts of entertainment had been organised for the children – boats, rafts, skin diving, ponies to ride, speedboats to tear up and down. All these delights were left untasted. The children seemed interested only in digging not in the sand but in the sticky clay dunes at the back of the beach. Questioned by affronted elders, the children said they were digging for the postman.

After a period of mystification it was recalled that thirty years ago a local postman disappeared under unusual circumstances. That is to say, at one moment he was standing alive and well in

> a public house and the next he was a corpse, apparently victim
> of hostile action and a moment or two later there was not even
> a corpse.

I have unfortunately not been able to find out the outcome of this case.

In December 1965, Thomas Cashin's son, also called Thomas, was involved in a bizarre dispute with a neighbour which was clearly influenced by his father's connection to the missing postman case. Thomas Cashin Jr and his wife Cherry lived in Ballyvadden, Kill, County Waterford. In 1964 their neighbours, Richard and Ann Walsh, fell out with them and started taunting the Cashins about the missing postman case, even going so far as to erect an effigy of a postman on a bicycle in their front garden for the purposes of annoying the Cashins. They were brought to court on a charge of harassing the Cashins but the case against Mr Walsh was struck out and the judge accepted an undertaking from Mrs Walsh not to interfere with the Cashins again. The judge described the whole episode as 'childish, silly and stupid'.

Four libel actions for £2,000 each were taken by four of the surviving former defendants in the missing postman case against the *Waterford News and Star* in May 1974. The plaintiffs were Thomas Cashin, James Whelan, Mrs Nora Orpen and George Cummins. The actions related to a review of the previously mentioned play *Prisoners of Silence*, written by James Cheasty and performed in Waterford's Theatre Royal in February 1972. The review had read as follows:

> Whatever may be said otherwise about James Cheasty's play 'Prisoners of Silence' at the Theatre Royal, Waterford, last week, it cannot be argued that its plot is not credible for there are people still around who remember vividly the real-life drama on which it is based. It happened in a County Waterford village over forty years ago and while Cheasty's play is not an exact replica, it is near enough to the real thing to be recognisable.
>
> The most frightening aspect is the fact that all its principal characters – men and women of substance – who should not have been in the pub on Christmas Day, all combined to get rid of the body rather than face the consequences and social stigma of illicit drinking.
>
> On the face of it, it seems hard to imagine otherwise respectable people would be prepared to go to such lengths as the disposal of a body to cover up the fact that they were drinking in the pub during prohibited hours, but everyone knows that such things had happened in real life Ireland. That is the kind of fear that James Cheasty was referring to in his programme note.

The plaintiffs claimed the article meant and was understood to mean that they had been guilty of the murder of Laurence Griffin and that they had conspired together and with others to conceal evidence to prevent the course of justice. They claimed that as a result of the article they had been held up to hatred, ridicule and contempt.

Solicitor Peter O'Connor reprised his role as the legal champion of the former defendants. The cases were settled for an undisclosed sum and the publishers apologised to the plaintiffs.

According to Dr Tadhg Ó Dúshláine's unpublished account of the missing postman case, Harry O'Mara continued to believe that he had been unjustly treated over the events in Stradbally, and often requested a public enquiry into the matter. When all these requests were refused:

> he eventually sent a copy of his testimony to *Irish Times* columnist Donal Foley, in the 1960s, in the hope that Foley would air the matter in his "Man Bites Dog" columns, in an attempt to get to the root of the saga. But Foley, being a Waterford man, had his ear to the ground and decided that, given the sensitivities still very much alive in this case, that discretion was the better part of valour.

In July 1977 the case of the missing postman was cited as part of the defence of Liam Townson, charged before the special criminal court with the murder of SAS captain and undercover agent Robert Nirac in South Armagh earlier that year. Conor Brady, the security correspondent of *The Irish Times*, got hold of the O'Mara statement which had been filed away ten years earlier by Donal Foley, and wrote a long feature based on it which appeared in the paper on 9 July 1977.

Within a month of the publication *The Irish Times* received a solicitor's letter sent on behalf of James Whelan and Mrs Nora Orpen, informing the paper of their intention to sue for libel:

> Our clients are the two surviving members of the Whelan family, and all the other persons charged with said murder with the exception, it is believed, of the two Guards Ned Dullea and Bill Murphy are dead. The said article ... is a most grave and serious libel on our clients' character and reputation and is made all the more grievous by the sensational manner in which the article is couched by you and the ghoulish description of the opening by the Guards of the graves in the local cemetery. You clearly took no steps to verify the facts before writing said article as if you did you would have ascertained:
>
> (a) That each and every one of the persons accused of the wilful murder of Larry Griffin including our respective clients made statements protesting their innocence and denying all knowledge of Laurence Griffin's death.
>
> (b) That the State did not withdraw the charges against our clients or the other accused persons but after protracted hearings at the District Court before the late Mr F. J. McCabe and after hearing learned Counsel on behalf of the state and

> the evidence the District Justice refused informations against our clients and the others accused holding that there was no case against them.
>
> (c) That no mention was made that James Fitzgerald the chief State Witness on being sworn repudiated the statement made by him to the Guards and was subsequently treated as a hostile witness and was not in fact believed by the Justice.

> The said article sets out in detail the said James Fitzgerald's statement as told to the court by state counsel Mr T. Finlay and no reference whatsoever is made to our clients' protests of their complete innocence.
>
> The article is a one-sided account of the affair and gives the distinct impression to any readers thereof that our clients were in fact guilty but could not be convicted due to lack of evidence.

The Irish Times received legal advice that James Whelan and Nora Orpen had a strong case and would probably be awarded substantial damages by a jury. The matter was settled out of court and in the words of Tadhg Ó Dúshláine, 'Harry O'Mara's testimony was again buried in the files of *The Irish Times*.'

Around 1988 the late writer and broadcaster Breandán Ó hEithir sent Tadhg Ó Dúshláine the draft outline of an anthology of Irish murders he was working on. He had already written the chapter on the case of the missing postman, which again drew heavily on former Superintendent Harry O'Mara's account. Ó hEithir recounted an experience he had had during the general election campaign of 1986 when he was employed by *The Irish Times* to write a daily sketchbook on the election in the hidden Ireland:

While in Waterford I came across a candidate who was campaigning for an unknown Christian Party on a bicycle. My efforts to catch up with him failed near Bunmahon and in the following day's sketchbook I reported that it would not be wise to ask anyone in the area if he had seen a man on a bike in view of what happened in the area in 1929.

That day I went through Stradbally on my way to Cork. It was early and Whelan's pub was not long open when I stopped my car on the other side of the road. I got out and stood looking at the pub ... A man came along the street reading the front page of *The Irish Times*. As he passed me I saluted him and as he replied he gave the double-take which signified recognition. My photograph appeared with the sketchbook every day and I am fairly well-known from my television days. The opportunity was too good to miss so I said: 'Was it upstairs or downstairs it happened?' He merely quickened his step, but when he was well away from me he tossed a remark over his shoulder in my general direction: 'I think it might be a good idea for you to fuck off out of here.'

As I drove away I noticed people coming to the door of the pub to engage the gentleman in conversation. Familiar as I am with the long Irish memory and the persistence of happenings long ago, it came as a shock to receive such a positive reaction to an event which occurred the month before I was born. It showed that things could never be the same in Stradbally.

Ó hEithir also recounted a late-night conversation he had with a man in a hotel in Dungarvan about 1976:

We talked of the missing postman and how it was that the mystery and the fantasies had obscured the real tragedy suffered by the widow and orphans. The man agreed and said that to make matters worse the poor postman was buried within a mile of his own house and that all the draining and the digging was caused by rumour deliberately spread at the behest of those who buried him. The man said that it was much too dangerous for anyone to go back to where he had been placed and that if I came with him he would tell me why, as well as show me the place.

He took his car and drove towards Kilmacthomas, telling me that part of the road was being tarmacadamed in 1929 and that only the soling (the large stones that were placed under the chips which were then tarred and steam-rolled) had been laid at a place where he would dip his lights, at the time of the disappearance. The body was concealed under the loose stones that night and was never moved at all. The County Council workers resumed work the day after St Stephen's Day and by the time the search had really intensified the steam-roller and the laying of the new surface had already moved on. What was there now was anyone's guess he said.

Where he dipped his lights, but would under no circumstances stop the car – although it was past midnight – I could not now pinpoint with any accuracy. It was dark, the road was not one with which I was familiar and a certain amount of drink was consumed during the evening.

Shortly afterwards Breandán Ó hEithir fell ill. He died three years later and his anthology of Irish murders never saw the light of day.

In the early 1990s the broadcaster Cathal O'Shannon tried to make a programme about the case of the missing postman for his RTÉ television series on Irish murders, *Thou Shalt Not Kill*. However, as he explained in a letter to Dr Tadhg Ó Dúshláine, RTÉ's lawyers shot down the proposal because James Whelan was still alive and was not, as we have seen, slow to sue for libel. O'Shannon also wrote that when he was researching the case 'I was almost run out of Stradbally and received two threats of legal action from the Whelan family.' O'Shannon requested, but was refused, permission to see the garda files on the case. Starting in 1990, Dr Tadhg Ó Dúshláine himself spent many years writing to various Ministers for Justice seeking access to the garda files but all his requests were refused.

Chapter 23

———✦———

The shadow of the missing postman case hung over Stradbally and many of its inhabitants for the rest of their lives. Some dealt well with its legacy, others were not so fortunate.

THE GRIFFIN FAMILY

Amidst all the lies, conflicting theories and controversies surrounding the case of the missing postman, it is easy to forget the human tragedy at the heart of the story. Not only was Larry's widow Mary left without her lifelong companion, but the failure to find the body greatly increased her distress. The few references we find to her state of mind following her husband's disappearance portray a woman grieving deeply and yearning desperately for her husband's remains to be returned to her. 'If I could only get his poor body for Christian burial, it would be the greatest comfort to me,' said Mrs Griffin to a reporter from the *Waterford Weekly Star* at the end of February 1930. At the beginning of April 1930 she was greatly upset by an untrue report which was published in another Waterford newspaper and also in an English newspaper to the effect that she had instructed her solicitors to enter an application to presume the death of her husband. 'I most emphatically deny having instructed my solicitors as suggested in that report,' she stated. 'I have not even contemplated taking such action, for I am confident God will hear my prayers and that my poor husband's body will be recovered for me to give him Christian burial.' In February 1931 Mary Griffin eventually applied for and was granted permission to presume the death of her husband and to apply for the administration of his estate.

Mrs Griffin clearly believed the Whelans, Cashin and the others were guilty of covering up her husband's death and disposing of his body and she cooperated with the *Cork Examiner* legal team in their defence of a libel action taken against the paper by the Whelans in June 1930, volunteering to give evidence on the newspaper's behalf.

Adding to Mary Griffin's emotional distress was the fact that she had lost her main source of income – Larry's weekly wages which were stopped the day he disappeared. However, the fund set up to assist the family eventually collected over £200 which was about the same as a postman's annual salary. The fund was very strongly supported by the people of Kilmacthomas, and there was a huge response from post-office staff all over Ireland. Apart from the nuns in the convent and the priests of the parish, however, there were very few contributions from the village of Stradbally in spite of Larry Griffin's many years of service there.

Mary Griffin's financial situation would have improved somewhat in 1935 with the introduction of the widow's state pension. She was also fortunate that her children were by then mostly grown up and were soon able to earn their own wages.

But the disappearance and presumed death of her husband was not to be the last tragedy in Mary Griffin's life. In 1933 her daughter Alice and their neighbour Dolly Whitty both died of pneumonia having received a soaking and been out in the cold while cycling to a football match in Dungarvan. Then in early May 1947, Mary's sixty-five-year-old brother Michael Fitzgerald and her twenty-nine-year-old nephew John left their small farm at Lisselty near Brownstown Head, County Waterford, to go lobster fishing in their small boat. A fairly strong easterly wind was blowing at the time and the water was choppy. Neither man ever returned home and subsequent searches failed to find any trace of them. Their bodies were washed ashore about a month later, however. It was presumed that their fifteen-foot boat capsized and that the men were thrown into the water.

Larry and Mary's son Jack trained as a mechanic and in 1932 he opened a motor-garage business in Kilmacthomas in partnership with another man called Paddy Lennon. It was a good time to get into the garage business as car ownership steadily increased in the following decades. The business flourished and Jack took sole ownership of it in 1966.

Jack married Bridie O'Connell from Ballygarron, Bunmahon,

in 1947. The postman's widow lived with the young couple for a few years and Bridie got to know her mother-in-law quite well. Bridie says that Mary often spoke to her about the missing postman case:

> She'd go through every detail of it. She was a very strong woman. As you can imagine she felt very bad about it and she was in deep shock for a while. She used to get these letters from time to time telling her that his body was in certain places. She used to tell the guards and they used to follow that up but nothing happened. Until she died she had hopes that he'd be found.

Mary Griffin died in 1958 at the age of eighty-three and was buried in the family plot in Newtown cemetery. Even though her husband's body is not in the grave, he is commemorated on the headstone: 'In loving memory of Larry Griffin, Kilmacthomas, died at Stradbally 25 December 1929'. Jack Griffin, who was nineteen when his father disappeared, remained deeply affected by the tragedy for the rest of his life and Christmas always brought back sad memories for him. Jack died on 18 April 1983.

Jack's widow Bridie still works in the family business in Kilmacthomas along with her two sons William and Leo, grandchildren of Larry Griffin. Bridie and Jack also had a daughter, Marion, who sadly passed away in London shortly before the publication of this book. At ninety years of age,

Bridie Griffin is a remarkably fit, healthy and sprightly woman, who was of great assistance both in the writing of this book and in the production of the *CSÍ* television programme which preceded it. She and her children are still haunted by the knowledge that Larry Griffin's body lies somewhere, probably not too far from them, and they feel a sense of obligation to Larry, Mary and Jack to keep his memory alive. While all those who were involved with Larry's disappearance have now passed away, the hope lingers that the knowledge of where his body rests was passed on to some person or persons still living, and that someone's conscience could finally be moved to yield up the final secret of the missing postman.

The memory of Larry Griffin also lived on among another branch of his descendents in County Mayo. Larry and Mary's daughter Bridie returned to her work in Manchester after the failure to solve the missing postman case and it was there she met Tom Mulrennan from Ballyhaunis. The couple married in 1946 and returned to Mayo in 1949 when Tom's father died, to look after his mother and the family farm. They had two children: Marie, born in 1948 in Manchester, and Seamus, born in 1950 in Ballyhaunis. Seamus Mulrennan says that he and his sister had very little knowledge of the missing postman story when they were growing up because their mother never spoke about it. It was clear to him, however, that it had a devastating effect on her:

It was something that was there in the background all the time. My mother and her mother and my uncle were looking for answers to it. The main thing was to get hold of the body, if they could just get hold of the body and give it a Christian burial.

Seamus and his sister Marie, like the Griffins of Kilmacthomas, also believe that there will be no sense of closure in the case of Larry Griffin until his body is found and interred in Newtown cemetery along with his beloved wife Mary.

JIM FITZGERALD

Very little is known about Jim Fitzgerald's life after the missing postman case, but what little I have been able to find out suggests that life was hard and lonely for him. Even though he had recanted his evidence on the stand, there was no future in Stradbally for a labouring man who had accused some of the most powerful people in the village of a terrible crime. He was in effect exiled from his home, and left Stradbally with little more than the clothes on his back. We know that Superintendent Hunt initially arranged employment for him with a farmer in County Galway. Some years later, according to local folklore, a school inspector from Stradbally called Thomas Flynn entered a hotel in Galway and got talking to a man who was sweeping the yard. He noticed that the man spoke with a Waterford accent and when he asked him where he was from he replied 'Stradbally'. Flynn then asked him his name and he replied 'Jim Fitzgerald'. However, Flynn did not realise who he was talking to because he did not know Fitzgerald personally, and only knew of him by the name 'Greaney' as Fitzgerald was known in Stradbally. It was only after returning to Stradbally and discussing the encounter with local people that he realised who he had met.

A local Stradbally man remembers Jim Fitzgerald coming back to Stradbally one last time in his old age. The local man's parents had been neighbours of Fitzgerald when he lived in Stradbally. He thinks this happened in the 1950s: 'I was here one day and the next thing this fella came up the road in a hackney and he came up to the door crying and my mother recognised him and threw her hands around him.' It may be, however, that this incident happened in 1945, for the records of the Little Sisters of the Poor in Waterford show that Jim Fitzgerald entered their home for the elderly poor in that year. Fitzgerald may have returned to Stradbally to get his baptismal records from the parish priest, as the nuns would have required this information. Jim Fitzgerald's entry in the Little Sisters' register contains only the sparsest details of his life: the names of his parents, Patrick Fitzgerald and Mary Foley; his place of birth and date of birth; his pension-book number; his marital status. However, under the heading 'Observations' there are two words which suggest that the shadow of the missing postman case hung over Jim Fitzgerald for the rest of his days, two words which sum up the tragedy of this poor labouring man's life: 'no friends'.

The Little Sisters' register records that Jim Greaney Fitzgerald died in their care on 4 December 1961.

TOMMY CORBETT

Tommy Corbett and his wife Bridget remained in Jim Fitzgerald's old labourer's cottage, although Tommy spent some time working in England. The land-registry records show that Tommy obtained outright ownership of the cottage in 1965. He died in 1968 aged sixty-three and his wife Bridget died in 1975 aged sixty-six. They were survived by their two children Billy and Chrissy.

THE WHELAN FAMILY

The publican Patrick Whelan kept his business afloat with the help of income from his various libel actions arising out of the missing postman case. He died in 1946 and his wife Bridget lived on until 1961. The family business was inherited by James, who died in 1997 aged eighty-seven years. The pub was then inherited and is currently owned and run by John Whelan, a son of James. Nora Whelan married and became Mrs Nora Orpen. She and her husband bought a pub in Knockboy near Ballygunner and had two daughters and a son. Nora passed away in 1987. Cissie Whelan married Johnny O'Brien, a schoolteacher in Goresbridge, County Kilkenny, and had a large family. She had more than her share of tragedy, however. Two of her sons died in infancy. In 1994 one of her grandsons, Cathal O'Brien, and another young man living in the same house in Wellington Terrace, Cork, disappeared, apparently having been beaten to death. A third man later disappeared from the same house, also presumed murdered. No one was ever convicted in relation to Cathal O'Brien's death and his body was never found. His suspected murderer, Frederick Flannery, took his own life in 2003. Cissie's husband passed away in 1995 at the age of seventy-nine and another of her sons, John, died in a motor accident in Chicago in 1996 at the age of fifty-three. Cissie Whelan herself passed away in 2004, at the age of ninety-four, and is buried in Skeoughvosteen, County Kilkenny, along with her husband, the three sons who predeceased her and yet another son, Philip, who passed away at the age of fifty-seven only one year after his mother's death.

A descendant of one of the Whelans in this book emailed me after the broadcast of the *CSÍ* programme asking me to recommend resources they could use to find out more information about the story of the missing postman. 'Even within the family it was a very underplayed issue,' the descendant wrote. 'In fact I knew very little about it until a short while ago.'

THOMAS CASHIN

After his reinstatement as principal of Ballylaneen National School, just as in the years before his arrest, Thomas Cashin continued to get poor reports on his work from Department of Education inspectors. He was rated 'non-efficient' as a teacher from 1931 until 1940 and was given many warnings that his standard of teaching needed to improve. He seems to have made no further effort to obtain an Irish-language qualification and was denied a salary increment every year until 1940. However, in that year, at the age of fifty-one, he finally managed to obtain an efficient rating for the first time since 1924. We don't know how he fared after that for there is no documentation in Cashin's file for subsequent years.

Thomas Cashin continued to play a prominent role in the local community for many years. A newspaper report from 1944 indicates that he had become involved in the local Fianna Fáil cumann. Thomas Cashin and his wife Kathleen retired from Ballylaneen National School in 1957, when the school itself closed its doors for the last time. Kathleen Cashin died in 1969 and Thomas Cashin died in 1976 aged eighty-six. He was survived by eight children, one of whom still lives in the house in Stradbally. I received no response to my efforts to contact this person in relation either to the *CSÍ* television programme or to this book.

NED MORRISSEY

The gravedigger Morrissey died in the 1960s and is buried in Stradbally cemetery, in a grave marked only by an iron cross with no inscription. His wife is buried in a different part of the same graveyard. They were survived by several children.

EX-GARDA EDWARD DULLEA

After his dismissal, ex-Garda Dullea returned to his home place at Gloun, Lisbealad, Dunmanway. According to the files, the local gardaí kept an 'unobtrusive watch' on him in the hope that they might pick up some information in relation to the missing postman case. In June 1930 Dullea wrote to local TD Jasper Wolfe, asking for his assistance in getting him reinstated in the force. Wolfe made unsuccessful representations on his behalf to the Minister for Justice. Dullea obtained a job as a store manager at a local creamery and when he was in his late sixties he married a former nurse.

A relative of Edward Dullea told me that he never heard him speaking about the case of the missing postman, 'but we heard about it growing up and it was always there in the background'. The same relative expressed the opinion that the gardaí 'came down very hard on him over what happened', and that what had happened 'was probably an accident'. He was dissatisfied with the depiction of Dullea in the *CSÍ* television programme: 'That's not the man we knew. He was a good man.' Another relative of Ned Dullea was also angry about the *CSÍ* programme, and he rang RTÉ on the morning of the broadcast asking that Dullea's name be removed from the programme. Ned Dullea died in 1987.

EX-GARDA WILLIAM MURPHY

After his discharge ex-Garda William Murphy returned to his native Bruree, County Limerick, where he was known either as Bill Murphy or by the nickname 'Blueball'. He returned to his former occupation of carpenter, making butter boxes in the local creamery. Like all former IRA men recruited to An Garda Síochána at the founding of the force, Murphy came from the pro-Treaty side and would have been a Cumann na nGaedheal supporter. However, as a result of being thrown out of the force, he switched allegiances and became a stalwart Fianna Fáil activist, falling out with many of his own relatives in the process. According to a neighbour in Bruree, Murphy used to say that he would get his job in the gardaí back if Fianna Fáil came to power. However, even after Fianna Fáil won the 1932 election Murphy was not reinstated.

In the early 1940s Murphy started his own business buying and selling turf, eggs, poultry and rabbits. One of his suppliers was Jimmy Collins who went on to be a TD for West Limerick from 1948 to 1967. Murphy and Collins became close friends and political allies. At the local cumann meetings some party member, not knowing about William's connection to the missing postman case, would propose him as a party candidate in the local elections, but Jimmy Collins would defuse the situation by saying that Murphy was too valuable to the organisation as a backroom organiser. Jimmy Collins was the father of Gerry Collins, the former Fianna Fáil TD and minister.

William Murphy was very active in local Gaelic Athletic Association circles, and he trained local hurling and camogie teams. He was also known in Bruree as a very religious man and was a leading member of the local confraternity of the Sacred Heart. However, even religion was affected by Civil War politics in Bruree. In those days when a dead person was brought to church the evening before the funeral mass, it would be a lay person and not a priest who would lead the congregation in saying the rosary. William Murphy used to perform this duty but only for funerals of Fianna Fáil supporters! Another local man, Dick Harris, looked after Cumann na nGaedheal funerals and yet another man, Jerry O'Regan, gave out the rosary for 'neutrals'.

In 1952, as outlined in Chapter 22, he and ex-Garda John Sullivan took a libel action against an English publication, the *Empire News*, over an article which repeated the theory that Griffin had died in the garda barracks.

After the war Murphy became a building contractor, starting off by building a few houses and gradually winning bigger contracts. This business failed, however, in the mid-1960s.

When he was nearly sixty years of age, Murphy married the local pension officer Eileen Curtin, who had a small farm which Murphy looked after when his building business collapsed.

Sonny Ward was a close neighbour of William Murphy in Bruree. According to Sonny, Murphy once told Sonny's father that he was upstairs in Whelan's with Nora Whelan when the postman was killed downstairs. Apart from that he never spoke about the missing postman case. Sonny himself was very close to William in later years and hoped that he would open up to him about the missing postman case, but William Murphy died suddenly in 1984 at the age of eighty-three without telling what he knew.

EX-GARDA PAT FRAWLEY

Ex-Garda Pat Frawley and his family remained in Stradbally after the missing postman case, and there seems to have been some sympathy for him in the area. In March 1933 the Bunmahon Fianna Fáil cumann unanimously passed a motion requesting the Minister for Justice to investigate his case with a view to having him reinstated in the force, but nothing came of their efforts. Then in 1937 Frawley became entangled in another case in which a Stradbally-based garda was charged with murder. Garda John Daly, from the same parish in County Clare as Frawley, was posted to Stradbally garda barracks, and he and Frawley struck up a friendship. On the night of 31 July

1937 Frawley and Daly went angling on the River Tay in the Woodhouse estate near Stradbally. Frawley had a sporting rifle with him. While they were fishing, a boy who was with another group of anglers came and told Daly: 'I think Tom Fitzgerald is poaching in the river.' Members of the Fitzgerald family had several previous convictions for poaching, and that night Tom was out drag-netting the river with his brother Michael. Michael was a sailor in the British navy at home on leave in Stradbally. Garda Daly took Patrick Frawley's rifle from him and went off in pursuit of the poachers. A short while later, witnesses heard Garda Daly shout 'Hi!' and then a shot rang out. Daly had shot dead Michael Fitzgerald who was unarmed, but Daly's defence was that the poacher had acted as if he was about to draw a gun on him and that he had fired in self-defence. This was disputed by Tom, the only other witness to the shooting. Garda Daly was charged with murder and tried in the Central Criminal Court in Dublin in November 1937. However, the jury accepted his evidence that he had acted in self-defence: he was found not guilty and resumed his duties as a member of An Garda Síochána at Stradbally.

Sometime after the Garda Daly murder case, the Frawley family moved from Stradbally to the Ferrybank area of Waterford city and Patrick Frawley obtained employment with Clover Meats Ltd. He died in 1954 in St Patrick's Hospital, Waterford, at the age of fifty-nine. He was survived by his widow Brigid, three daughters and a son. An obituary in the *Munster Express* described him as 'a widely-known figure' who 'was held in much esteem by a wide circle of friends'.

EX-GARDA SERGEANT JAMES CULLINANE

After his discharge James Cullinane returned to his home place at Caherbeg, Rosscarbery, County Cork, where he worked on the family farm with his brother Mick. His courtship of Patrick Frawley's sister-in-law was not rekindled and he remained unmarried. According to neighbours and relatives, the feeling in the locality was that he had been wronged and that he should not have been thrown out of the guards. One relative told me that his dismissal from the force 'broke his heart', although he did not talk about it much. In 1938 his health started to fail as a result of 'a growth in his stomach' according to the garda files. The gardaí at Rosscarbery, being aware that he was dying, kept in close touch with him with a view to finding out any information which he may have had concerning the disappearance of Larry Griffin. But nothing transpired to indicate that he had new information which he had failed to impart at any stage of the investigations. Jim Cullinane died on 12 February 1939.

EX-GARDA JOHN SULLIVAN

John Sullivan, his wife and his two young children continued to live in Stradbally for some months after his dismissal from the force, but he had no means of supporting his family. It is clear that Sullivan harboured a deep sense of injustice over his dismissal from the force and almost immediately began appealing to the garda commissioner for his reinstatement. Many of these letters survive in the garda files. In July 1930, three months after his discharge, Sullivan wrote to General O'Duffy that he was 'directed by Fr Leo of the Passionist Fathers who is on a Mission here to apply again to you to be re-instated'. He received a reply on behalf of the commissioner stating that 'recruiting is closed by order of the government and is unlikely to be resumed for some considerable time'.

The financial situation of the family was now getting desperate, and in September 1930 solicitor J. F. Williams of Dungarvan, acting on behalf of Sullivan, wrote to An Garda Síochána seeking a refund of pension money deducted from his pay during the period while he was a member of the force. A senior officer wrote back to Williams to inform him that 'in the case of members who are dismissed these monies are not refunded to the members themselves, but may, with the consent of the Minister for Finance, be applied for the benefit of their wives and children'. Williams then made an application on behalf of Mrs Bridget Sullivan and her two children for the pension money. He indicated that John Sullivan was still unemployed and that the money would be 'very useful for the support and maintenance of his wife and children'. The application was successful and the pension money, which amounted to £24 6s 4d, was refunded to the family.

In October 1930, John Sullivan and his family moved to London to try to obtain employment. However, they continued to struggle financially, and after a while the children were sent back to Ireland to live with their grandparents in County Cavan. In March 1933, Sullivan wrote from London to O'Duffy's successor as garda commissioner, Colonel Eamon Broy, seeking reinstatement. He pointed out that he had been dismissed from the force without any charge being brought against him:

> I should at least have a fair trial after six years service in the gardaí and two years in the army. I would also like to let you know that after being dismissed I done all in my power to get information concerning the case. I found out the exact time the man was killed and the names of some of those present at the time. The School Teacher got back his job after twelve months. I think I should get mine seeing I was never charged with any offence.

Again, however, he received a reply stating that it was not possible to consider his readmission to the force because recruiting had been entirely suspended by order of the government for over a year and there were no indications of a resumption in the near future.

In June 1933 Sullivan made another desperate appeal for reinstatement:

I came over here to London to try and earn a living last October two years. Ever since I can't say I done more than eighteen months work. I must depend on my wife to support me. Our two children are over in Ireland as we could not afford to keep them here. I can't get a constant job. I went after a good job this morning and would have got it were it not for my discharge. He would not believe me when I told him I was never charged with any offence but just dismissed. I would have been in the LBB trams last March were it not for the same thing, so you see I am down as a criminal without any chance of proving my case. I have had three years of hardship for no reason of my own but if I am not back in the Force before that three years is up I am going back to Dublin when the new government assemble and make them give me a hearing ... I will keep at it until I get justice.

I have not found any evidence that Sullivan did travel to Dublin to 'make' the new Fianna Fáil government give him a hearing, and it is unlikely that he would have been successful in demanding access to government ministers.

In late 1933 or early 1934, Sullivan had to return to his parents' small farm on Bere Island to help his father look after his sick mother. However, his wife stayed on in London trying to earn some money and the children remained in County Cavan with their grandparents. In February 1934, Sullivan again sought reinstatement in An Garda Síochána: 'It is very hard on me after all my service in both Volunteers and National

Army to be out of a job now and my wife and children separated after all this time.' Sullivan had heard that Ned Dullea had been reinstated in the gardaí and he wrote: 'I think I should have a better claim than him as he was charged with the murder of the Postman.' However, Sullivan was misinformed on this point, for Dullea was never reinstated in the force. Sullivan promised the commissioner that if 'you re-instate me I will be a policeman both by word and deed as I have learned a very hard lesson since I was dismissed nearly four years ago'.

In July 1934, John Sullivan tried a different approach, writing to the garda commissioner that 'there will not be any legal action taken on my behalf or by me with regard to my dismissal if I am reinstated'. His implied threat of legal action had no effect, however, and in reality there was little likelihood of success in such a course of action. He made several more applications for reinstatement over the following years, and even though An Garda Síochána had begun recruiting again, all his applications were turned down. Unsuccessful representations were also made on his behalf by a senator, a TD and other third parties up to about 1940.

Sullivan's wife and family eventually joined him on Bere Island, and the family began to make the best of their situation. They had two further children, Mary born in 1936 and Seán born in 1938. While the parents clearly found it hard to adjust to their new circumstances, even the oldest children did not really remember any other kind of life. Pauline, who was only two years old at the time of the missing postman case, remembers an idyllic childhood on Bere Island:

> Dad fished from the rocks, caught rabbits, taught me to fish and shoot – nowadays it would be called 'the good life'! We always had our own milk, butter, potatoes and carrots – stored in sand for winter use and lots of cabbage in spring. There was plenty of fish, rabbits and chickens. My mother made her own bread, butter, and jars of blackberry and apple jam. My mother was a wonderful provider from her kitchen garden to create an all-year-round supply of fruit and veg – salads, onions, rhubarb and gooseberries in plenty. The Cavan grandparents' farm supplied Christmas goose and Santa's presents.

Pauline's father earned some extra money doing maintenance work at the Irish army base on Bere Island.

Pauline says that her mother was very religious and that she had a long-held belief that those responsible for Larry Griffin's death and disappearance would admit what they knew before they died: 'We prayed for them and their families every day after supper when saying the rosary – I do not know what good it did.'

In 1954 John Sullivan won an undisclosed sum of damages, of the order of several hundred pounds, in the previously mentioned libel action he took in conjunction with ex-Garda Murphy against the *Empire News*.

Interestingly, his father's history proved no barrier to

Pauline's brother Seán being accepted into An Garda Síochána and he went on to have a successful career, retiring at the rank of sergeant.

John Sullivan died on Bere Island in 1980 and his wife Bridget died there in 1994. Their daughter Pauline left Bere Island in 1947 and went to live in England and is now known by her married name, Pauline Clifford. She became interested in the missing postman case when she read an article about it in *The Irish Times* in January 2006: 'I felt rather sad that at no time did any one of us try to find out what had happened to the Postman's children.' In August 2006 Pauline visited Stradbally and took tea in Whelan's pub:

> There were four men sat at the bar and I asked if this was the pub that the postman departed from at Christmas 1929? They put their fingers to their mouths and tried to hush me up but I went into 'free-flow' and told them who I was.

Pauline has been very helpful to me in my research for this book, and has been more open about the missing postman case then many of the relatives of those connected with the story. While she believes that her father was not directly involved in Larry Griffin's death and disappearance – and I conclude in this book that she is correct in that belief – she acknowledges that his behaviour at the time was not without fault.

In retirement Pauline and her husband now spend as much

time as possible on Bere Island in a house they built there a few years ago. Her eldest brother also still lives on the island.

HARRY O'MARA

Even though Chief Superintendent O'Mara had been banished to Donegal he believed that General O'Duffy and Deputy Commissioner Coogan continued to victimise him. He wrote later that he had been informed 'on very reliable authority' that General O'Duffy proposed dismissing him from the force with ignominy and that, if it had not been for the strong attitude adopted by one of the assistant commissioners in his defence, this would have been done 'without the semblance of a trial or without having had the opportunity of making a statement'. However, with General O'Duffy's dismissal in 1933 by the new Fianna Fáil administration, O'Mara's fortunes within the force began to improve. In that year he was transferred to Castlebar in County Mayo and in 1935 he moved to Tralee, County Kerry, where he served until 1946. He was evidently very happy there for he chose to return in his retirement. In 1946 he took charge of the garda depot in the Phoenix Park, a clear sign that he was back in favour at the top level of the force. O'Mara also became very active in Catholic organisations. He organised and was chief marshal of large Pioneer Total Abstinence Association rallies at Croke Park in 1949 and 1959. He led a pilgrimage of more than a hundred gardaí and their families to Rome in 1955 where he presented Pope Pius XII with a cheque for £500 for the missions. In 1953 he led a garda pilgrimage to Fatima, during which he was received in Madrid by the dictator General Franco. He was president for a number of years of the Federation of Catholic Schools Unions and also of the Handball Association of Ireland. He was also the founder and chairman of a Garda Boys Club at Finglas, County Dublin. His last posting was to Mullingar and he retired from the force in January 1961. He then bought the Grand Hotel in Tralee, County Kerry, and moved to live in that town. He died in October 1969 and was survived by two sons and two daughters.

SUPERINTENDENT JAMES HUNT

Superintendent Hunt transferred from Galway to Callan, County Kilkenny, in 1933. He moved to Easkey, County Sligo, in 1937 and to Enniscrone, County Sligo, in 1940. He retired from the force in 1946 on grounds of ill health and went to live in Ballyhaunis, County Mayo, in his wife Mary's native county. Coincidently, this was also the area where one of Larry Griffin's daughters went to live having married a Mayo man. When Mrs Hunt died in 1972 James went to live with his daughter Maureen in Derry city. He died in Derry in 1978 and is buried in Ballyhaunis. He was survived by eight of his nine children.

EX-GARDAÍ PATRICK McNAMARA, JOSEPH GANTLEY, JAMES DRISCOLL AND THOMAS O'ROURKE

By contrast with the feeling towards the five dismissed Strad-bally gardaí, there was a lot of sympathy in the force for the four officers who had been forced to resign having lost the case taken against them by Tommy Corbett. In the dying days of the Cumann na nGaedheal administration, after losing the 1932 election, the government agreed to a request from General O'Duffy that the four men be reinstated in the force. But after the handover of power, Fianna Fáil members in the Waterford area attempted to have the men dismissed again on the basis that they had participated actively in the recent election campaign on the Cumann na nGaedheal side, and that they had torn down Fianna Fáil posters. The new Minister for Justice, James Geoghegan, ordered General O'Duffy to investigate the allegations. The investigation found that McNamara, O'Rourke and Gantley had been involved on the Cumann na nGaedheal side in the election campaign, but found no evidence that they had torn down Fianna Fáil posters. Driscoll had been at home in West Cork during the election and took no active part in the campaign. General O'Duffy, in reporting the findings of the investigation to the minister, strongly defended the actions of the men:

It is only fair to say … that at this period they were no longer attached to the Force, they were in a very bad way financially, and were willing to take any employment they could get. They were in fact – particularly those of them who had no friends with whom they could live – practically down and out. Some of them had a short period of employment during the Election – such casual work as fell to several others – and they were glad to get some small remuneration. They got very little … They appear to have been very restrained, and to have acted in self preservation. They had no influence and no friends, and should not be judged harshly.

O'Duffy also argued that the events that led up to their dismissal from the force had no political significance: 'They were the victims of circumstances, and were in my opinion treated unjustly. During my ten years' service as commissioner they were the only members dismissed whom I considered should not be dismissed.' Quite apart from O'Duffy's opinion that officers who had beaten up a witness should not have been dismissed in the first place, it is hard to see how the men's legitimate involvement as civilians in an election campaign before their reinstatement could have been grounds for their dismissal a second time.

The Minister for Justice does not seem to have pursued the matter, despite the political pressure from members of his own party. There was already more than enough tension between the new government and most of the senior members of An Garda Síochána. As Conor Brady writes: 'The men whom, only six brief years earlier they had tracked down, persecuted, arrested and imprisoned, were now their political masters.'[3] The new Minister for Justice, James Geoghegan, was a mild-mannered barrister, and one of the few members of the new cabinet who was not a recently converted gunman. He may have considered it prudent not to be overly vindictive with the force, although ironically, within a year and after another election which consolidated Fianna Fáil's grip on power, General O'Duffy himself was dismissed by de Valera's government.

Meanwhile the four officers went on to have long and successful careers in the force. Inspector Patrick McNamara was promoted to superintendent in 1940, served in the Cork, Carlow/Kildare and Sligo/Leitrim garda divisions, and died while still a member of the force in 1954. Joseph Gantley served at garda HQ and various stations in Longford and Westmeath, before returning to garda HQ, where he retired in 1958. He died in 1973. James Driscoll spent the rest of his career in Dublin and was decorated with the award of Comhairle na Mire Gaile in 1953. He retired in 1965. Garda Thomas O'Rourke was posted to Cork city after his reinstatement. On 6 November 1932 he and two colleagues were called to the scene of a house fire at Blackrock Road. What happened next is recounted in the book *An Garda Síochána and the Scott Medal* by Gerard O'Brien:

---

3   Brady (1974), p. 162

When they arrived they were loudly called upon by a gathered crowd to save the life of a man believed trapped upstairs by the flames. The three gardaí forced open the front door and Garda O'Rourke immediately made his way to the kitchen, where he soaked his handkerchief prior to making his way upstairs. After a search fraught with danger (nobody was actually in the house after all) Garda O'Rourke was overcome by smoke and heat and barely made his way back to the front door before he collapsed. Thereafter he spent over three weeks in hospital and it was a further month before he was fit to return to duty.[4]

Thomas O'Rourke was awarded a Scott Bronze Medal for his bravery in this incident. He was promoted to sergeant in 1942, to inspector in 1961 and to superintendent in 1964. As well as serving in Cork, he also spent periods in the Sligo/Leitrim, Louth/Meath, Mayo and Tipperary divisions. He retired in 1968 and died in March 1992.

---

4   O'Brien (2008), p. 44

Chapter 24

⟫●⟪

In February 2009 the team in *Cláracha Gaeilge* (Irish-language programmes) at RTÉ television started work on a new series about historical crime cases called *CSÍ* and I was assigned to work on the case of the missing postman.

My enquiries soon brought me into contact with Dr Tadhg Ó Dúshláine of Roinn na Gaeilge, NUI Maynooth, who had been interested for many years in the missing postman case from a folklore point of view. I was also directed towards Seán Murphy of Kilmacthomas, whose father Mike had replaced Larry Griffin as postman on the Stradbally route. I found important documentation in a Department of Justice file on the missing postman case held in the National Archives, and my colleague Margaret Martin got hold of some of the most important witness statements in the case of the missing postman. I also obtained Chief Superintendent O'Mara's personal account of the missing postman case. The relatives of Larry Griffin – the Griffins in County Waterford and the Mulrennans in County Mayo – came on board in the hope that new information would emerge about the case which might help solve the mystery of what happened to his body.

While the witness statements we had in our possession were fascinating, particularly Jim Fitzgerald's account of Larry Griffin's death, it was clear that they were only a part of a larger file. This file had been kept hidden away from the public for many years for sound legal reasons. But now that all those involved in the case had passed on, surely there could be no objection to giving the Griffin family some of the answers they wanted? There was also the question of the physical evidence which the gardaí had collected in the missing postman case. Dr Tadhg Ó Dúshláine had information that there were several boxes of material relating to the case in garda HQ, and he was convinced that these boxes must contain the physical evidence. The information gleaned from the forensic tests of 1930 had been of limited use in the missing postman case. At best those tests could only determine whether a particular substance was blood, and whether it was human or animal blood. But a modern DNA test could, for example, determine if particular bloodstains matched the blood of surviving members of the Griffin family.

Dr Ó Dúshláine had been refused access to the files on many occasions over the previous two decades. But now that the Griffin family themselves were appealing for the release of the information, perhaps, we thought, the case for full disclosure would be given a more sympathetic hearing. However, both the Griffins' and my requests were refused.

We proceeded with the filming and editing of the *CSÍ* programme on the basis of the documentation we had at our disposal, most of which was being revealed publicly for the first time. While we had not succeeded in getting access to the complete garda file for the purpose of the programme, the family hoped that the publicity surrounding the broadcast might help their campaign to have the file opened. They also hoped that someone in the vicinity of Stradbally might know where Larry Griffin's body had been hidden – perhaps having heard it from one of those involved before his or her death – and that the programme might stir their conscience to reveal what they knew.

As the date of the transmission approached there were various items about the programme in the print and broadcast media. Then, on the Friday before the Monday of the broadcast, Garda Commissioner Fachtna Murphy announced that the garda file on the Larry Griffin case would be made available for inspection in the Garda Museum. When I sought clarification, I was informed that the commissioner's order related to all materials held by An Garda Síochána in connection with the case – documents, photographs and physical items. The Griffin family were delighted, hopeful that the secrecy surrounding the case was finally coming to an end. It was arranged with the Garda Museum and Archives that I could inspect the file for the first time the morning after the broadcast of our programme.

On Tuesday morning, 15 September 2009, I visited the

Garda Museum in a state of anticipation and excitement. I quickly came down to earth when a single thin file was placed on a table in front of me. I was told that this was definitely all the material held by An Garda Síochána in relation to the missing postman case. In the normal course of events I would have had to accept this at face value. However, I already had in my possession various parts of the missing postman garda file which I had obtained from three different sources. Many of the documents I had already seen were not in this small file which had been placed before me. In other words, in spite of the garda commissioner's order, I had not been given the entire file on the case.

In the days that followed I corresponded with An Garda Síochána, pointing out to them that I knew for a fact that I had not been shown the entire file. I also talked about the matter on the *Today with Pat Kenny* show on RTÉ Radio 1. Larry Griffin's grandson Seamus Mulrennan also expressed his frustration and disappointment to An Garda Síochána over what had happened. After a number of days the garda archivist wrote to inform me that 'as a result of further enquiries' he had established the availability of further documentation consisting of nine files of documents and an album of photographs. The original single file had now grown to ten files and a photo album!

When I went to inspect these extra files, it was clear that they had not been recently recovered from some dusty archive where they had been stored away for many years. They were certainly not in their original covers – they had recently been refiled in modern file covers with labels which had been printed using a modern computer. There were thousands of pages in the files – I estimate between 5,000 and 10,000 – and all of the garda documents I had already seen were in this file. However, I was told that the gardaí did not have any of the physical evidence relating to the case and that there was no record of when it had been disposed of or what had happened to it.

The dramatic reconstructions in our RTÉ *CSÍ* television programme of the events leading to Larry Griffin's death had been based on Jim Fitzgerald's witness statement. Even though we made it clear on the television programme that these reconstructions were based on one man's testimony, it is fair to say that most people involved in the programme, including former Garda Detective Gerard Lovett, believed that the statement had a ring of truth about it. The only participant to sound a note of caution about the statement was the psychologist we interviewed for the programme, Dr Colm Ó Riagáin. 'In this case and in any case there's no clear line between the truth and lies,' said Dr Ó Riagáin.

In witness statements, you can expect half-lies, lies and misunderstandings. Therefore it's hard to analyse statements. Often members of the public and members of An Garda Síochána think that it's very easy to distinguish between someone who's telling the truth and someone who is lying. But the research on the subject shows that it's extremely difficult to make that differentiation and that often it's no better than guesswork.

As I began to trawl painstakingly through the newly released garda documents, I became aware of a major problem with Fitzgerald's statement – there was very strong evidence suggesting that he was elsewhere at the time he claimed to have been in Whelan's pub witnessing Larry Griffin's death. It also became clear to me that the gardaí themselves had never realised this problem with Fitzgerald's statement before they put him on the stand, and that they had never properly cross-checked the various witness statements they had collected, so convinced were they of the truthfulness of Fitzgerald's account. And yet I still hesitated to dismiss Fitzgerald, unable to understand how a country labourer could have fabricated a statement that was still so compelling eighty years later.

It was my eventual discovery among the thousands of garda documents of Superintendent Hunt's interviews with Fitzgerald in March 1930 that finally solved this mystery. Fitzgerald had not been in Whelan's when Larry Griffin died, but his statement was so convincing because it was based on an account he had heard from his lodger Tommy Corbett, who had in turn heard it from Patrick Cunningham, one of those who had been in the pub when the terrible event had happened.

Solving the mystery of Jim Fitzgerald's statement was

the key to unlocking the meaning of the thousands of often contradictory pieces of evidence in the missing postman case. It is this crucial discovery which now makes it possible for the first time in over eighty years to reconstruct the events of Christmas night 1929 in Stradbally. By 6 p.m. that evening Larry Griffin had finished his rounds. He had consumed far more alcohol than he was accustomed to due to the festive tradition of welcoming the postman with a drink. He met up with Garda Dullea in the centre of Stradbally, probably in the post office or just in front of it. Dullea had also been drinking, although he was not as drunk as Larry. Dullea and Larry went up to Garda Patrick Frawley's flat above the post office, possibly at Dullea's suggestion, where they got more drink. After a while Griffin and the two gardaí, Dullea and Frawley, came outside and stood in the square. Dullea and Frawley discussed what to do about Griffin, as he was too drunk to cycle home to Kilmacthomas. Frawley said he would go to Whelan's to see 'if the coast was clear' and to ask them would they put Larry up for the night. But Sergeant Cullinane spotted Frawley going into Whelan's. There was an ongoing problem with the gardaí in Stradbally barracks drinking in Whelan's pub and the sergeant suspected that was what Frawley was up to. The sergeant followed Frawley into the pub, prompting Frawley to make a hasty exit and come back to where Dullea and the postman were standing. But the sergeant had not recognised Dullea because he was in civvies and it was dark. So a while later Dullea and the postman headed off around Whelan's corner, Dullea pushing the bicycle and the postman leaning drunkenly on him for support. After they went around the corner they entered Whelan's by the back door.

Various other privileged members of the community were allowed into Whelan's that night for an illegal Christmas Day drinking session, including Thomas Cashin and Garda Murphy. All of those later arrested in connection with the case were there that night with the possible exception of Ned Morrissey. Later that night, Larry Griffin was involved in an altercation in Whelan's with Thomas Cashin, and possibly Ned Morrissey (if he was there) as well.

Some witnesses say they saw Ned Morrissey in his own house at 9 p.m. and Superintendent Hunt came to the conclusion that Morrissey was not in Whelan's that night. On the other hand, how did Morrissey come to feature so prominently in Fitzgerald's account, which was so convincing and detailed only because it was based on what he had been told by Tommy Corbett? While it is likely that some details may have changed in the telling, it seems unlikely that something as fundamental as who was involved in the altercation leading to Griffin's death would get mixed up. Furthermore, after Morrissey was arrested his wife was heard telling him: 'Remember Ned you have a tongue in your cheek and keep it there.' She also said to him that they were better off now than ever they were as the 'master's wife', meaning Mrs Cashin, was sending food and 'stuff' to the house. This suggests that Morrissey did know about what had happened that night, and that the Cashins had a vested interest in keeping him on side. It is my own opinion that, on the balance of probability, Morrissey was present in Whelan's that night and that he was involved in the altercation with Cashin.

What was the result of the altercation involving Griffin, Cashin and Morrissey? Three different scenarios are presented in the evidence. The least likely of these is that Griffin was badly injured having been knocked down and that he was taken away to be disposed of while still alive. This is the scenario that counsel for the prosecution suggested in court, and it was supposedly based on what Jim Fitzgerald told him that morning. If true, it would make the death of Larry Griffin cold-blooded murder. However, Jim Fitzgerald did not make this allegation in his original statement and there is not a shred of evidence anywhere else to support it.

The other two scenarios are both more credible. One is that Larry Griffin died instantly in Whelan's and that his body was removed from there by Cashin and others to be disposed of. The other is that the postman was brought over to the garda barracks by Gardaí Dullea and Murphy and put to bed there. Dullea and Murphy then returned to the pub. After some time the postman woke up, wandered out of bed still under the influence of alcohol and fell down the stairs to his death. Then perhaps Dullea or Murphy returned to check up on him, found him dead and returned to Whelan's to tell the others, whereupon it was decided to cover up his death and dispose of the body.

Whichever of these scenarios is nearest the truth, the motivations of those involved in the cover-up were the same – to protect their jobs and positions of relative power in the community. Patrick Whelan was already in dire financial difficulties and the loss of his pub licence would have been disastrous. It is difficult to see how the schoolteacher Cashin or the Gardaí Dullea and Murphy could have hoped to keep their jobs if it emerged that they had been present at an illegal drinking session which had resulted in a man's death. It was even worse for Cashin, as he had been directly involved in the altercation which had led to the postman being knocked down. Prosecutions would certainly have followed and while a murder conviction was unlikely, a manslaughter conviction was a real possibility. Regardless of the outcome of such a trial, the livelihoods and reputations of all those involved would have been destroyed beyond repair.

The consequences for the others present would not have been as serious. Men such as the labourer Tommy Corbett and the farmer Patrick Cunningham could have expected a conviction and a fine for drinking in a pub on Christmas Day, but nothing more serious as they had not been directly involved in the postman's death. However, it is not hard to see how they would have taken a lead from the likes of Thomas Cashin, the two gardaí and the Whelans. Cashin in particular was a person with leadership abilities, education and a known republican pedigree. Taking control of a situation such as this would have come naturally to him. As he had been a member of the IRA, and possibly still involved in it, he would have known how to make a body disappear, whether or not he had been personally involved in such an activity before.

The next question is where Larry Griffin's body was disposed of. It is possible that the body was moved from its initial resting place, and perhaps even moved several times. Gardaí Dullea and Murphy were not under suspicion during the earliest part of the investigation and would have been well placed to pre-empt garda searches of particular locations. Of course, if the body was disposed of in one of the mineshafts, there would be no possibility of moving it again. The mineshaft at Tankardstown can be ruled out as it was thoroughly searched. However, in spite of the weeks spent dragging the mineshaft at Ballinasisla, the gardaí were never able to say definitively that the postman's body had not been dumped there. The body could have been shifted from the bottom of the shaft by tidal waters into a subterranean channel out of reach of the grappling apparatus. It was too dangerous for a diver to descend to investigate this possibility. While writing the book, I discussed with underwater-survey expert Karl Bredendieck the possibility of exploring the mineshaft with a remote-control camera. But when Seán Murphy and I went in search of the actual location of Ballinasisla mineshaft, we discovered that it no longer exists. It has been thoroughly filled in and cows now graze on the exact spot where the opening to the shaft was once located. If Larry's body does lie in some subterranean tunnel at Ballinasisla, it is unlikely that it will ever be recovered.

The dominant theory in local folklore is that Larry Griffin's body is buried under the road near Ballyvoile Bridge, two and a half miles from Stradbally. According to this story, there were roadworks going on near the bridge at the time of the postman's disappearance or shortly afterwards. His body was buried under the roadworks in the middle of the night and unknowingly tarmacadamed over the next day by council workers. The Ballyvoile theory was well established in local folklore by the time Breandán Ó hEithir was looking into the missing postman story in the 1980s. But it does not appear at all in the garda files from the 1930s and, as we have seen in the course of this book, the gardaí took note in the files of local gossip and rumours as well as eyewitness accounts. The story should therefore be treated with caution. Even if Larry's body was buried under the road there would be only a small chance that it could be located using modern geophysical survey techniques. Ultimately the only way to check out this theory would be to entirely excavate a large section of roadway to a depth of several metres, an action that could hardly be justified on the basis of a folk theory of dubious veracity.

One of the aspects of this story that most amazes people

who hear it is that none of those who knew the location of the body ever revealed the secret, even on their deathbeds, in order to clear their consciences and do the right thing by the Griffin family. The first point that should be noted here is that many of those who were present in Whelan's pub may not have known exactly where the body was disposed of. This was probably arranged between a smaller group of people including Thomas Cashin and Gardaí Dullea and Murphy. Perhaps only those who travelled with the body in the car knew exactly where the body was disposed of. In Jim Fitzgerald's statement the body was placed in the back seat of the car. Thomas Cashin was the driver and Ned Morrissey sat in the front passenger seat. It makes sense that Thomas Cashin was the driver, as he owned the car, and there really was room for only one other person, whether that was Morrissey or someone else. The luggage compartment on motor cars of that era would not have been large enough to take a human body, so there would have been no room on the back seat for more passengers.

The other opinion to bear in mind about the body never being given up is that this is not as rare an occurrence as might be presumed. In the same series of *CSÍ* in which the missing postman story was broadcast, I worked on a programme about the killings of thirteen West Cork Protestants by elements of the anti-Treaty IRA in April 1922. The bodies of the first three to be killed, Thomas Hornibrook, Samuel Hornibrook and Captain Herbert Woods were secretly buried by a party of IRA men and have never been returned to their families. Even in the case of the more recent 'Troubles' in Ireland, several of the bodies of the 'disappeared' have never been returned to their families. In Ireland, those who know 'where the bodies are buried' can and do go to the grave without revealing their secret.

However, as Larry's grandson, Seamus Mulrennan points out:

This wasn't any anti-Treaty IRA killing. It wasn't a kidnapping nor was it a robbery. In fact it was a simple accident which could happen today in any pub anywhere. You would have thought Larry was in the safest possible place, in his friend's pub on Christmas night in the company of people he knew, the pillars of society and the local gardaí – people to whose houses he called every day. We are sure his wife Mary would have slept soundly that night if she had known where he was. What those friends and gardaí did to him and his family was a terrible deed. They denied him a Christian burial and they denied his family a chance to say goodbye and bury him in the family graveyard. Before they departed this world they could have let someone know where the body was. I doubt if there are many other cases like this.

Stradbally today is the type of well-kept, attractive country village that gets photographed for postcards and tourist guides of Ireland. The work of the local Tidy Towns committee is much in evidence in the well-maintained public areas and displays of bright flowering plants. Whelan's public house is still in business and is now run by John Whelan, a son of James and a grandson of Patrick. A daughter of Thomas Cashin still lives in his old house on the square. Some miles away in Kilmacthomas Larry's daughter-in-law Bridie and his grandsons Willie and Leo still live and work. Many other relatives of those involved in these events also still live in the area.

In many ways the story of the missing postman is the story of Ireland in recent times. Like so many other issues in the wider society, for many decades the story of Larry Griffin has been a taboo subject in Stradbally and the surrounding area. A book on the history of Stradbally which came out only a few years ago made no mention of the biggest story ever to happen there. A new generation has grown up who knew little or nothing about the story, because of the silence of their elders. The memory of the postman, just like his body, was buried and hidden away so that an uncomfortable reality would not have to be faced up to. For many years, even the Griffin family themselves repressed their awful tragedy, as so many victims of other abuses have done.

But now, finally, the secrecy and silence of the missing postman case is being challenged, not simply because I pursued the story, but also because the time was right to tell it. On a practical level I had access to documents which no one before could get hold of, and I did not have to worry about the threat of legal actions from those involved in the case. But more importantly, Irish people are no longer willing to accept the culture of secrecy and shame in their society. Members of the Griffin family have explicitly made the link between their desire for openness in Larry's case and the other dark secrets of church, state and society that have had the light of day shone on them in recent times. They have been happily surprised by the number of people in their locality who have come to speak to them about the story of Larry Griffin, in the aftermath of the *CSI* television programme. And while some of the direct relatives of those involved in the case are still hostile or uncooperative, many others in the village of Stradbally and elsewhere have helped me with this book. The desire for the truth to come out is strong but the fear has not totally gone away – most of those in Stradbally who helped me with this book asked that their contributions be kept anonymous.

The hope of the wider Griffin family now is that the more the story is talked about, the more the fear around it will be dispelled and the greater the chance that some information will come to light which will lead to the discovery of the body. I do not know if Larry's body will ever rest in the family plot in Newtown along with his beloved wife Mary. However, I hope that the very act of telling his story, of keeping his memory alive, is in itself a fitting memorial to the man who for so many years brought news from afar to so many people in Stradbally and the surrounding area.

Bibliography

BOOKS

Allen, Gregory, *The Garda Síochána – Policing Independent Ireland 1922–82* (Gill and Macmillan, Dublin, 1999)

Brady, Conor, *Guardians of the Peace* (Gill and Macmillan, Dublin, 1974)

Hickey, Tom, and John Keane, *Stradbally na Déise* (Stradbally Tourism and Enterprise Group, Stradbally, 2007)

McGarry, Fearghal, *Eoin O'Duffy – A Self-Made Hero* (Oxford University Press, Oxford, 2005)

O'Brien, Gerard, *An Garda Síochána and the Scott Medal* (Four Courts Press, Dublin, 2008)

Reynolds, Mairead, *A History of the Irish Post Office* (MacDonnell Whyte, Dublin, 1983)

NEWSPAPERS

Cork Examiner
Daily Express

Daily Mail

Daily Mirror

Empire News

Evening News

Irish Independent

The Irish Times

Munster Express

The Sunday Telegraph

Waterford News

Waterford News and Star

Waterford Weekly Star

OFFICIAL DOCUMENTS

Department of Education General Registry files, File 13001 Box 252 and
File 27034 Box 614, National Archives of Ireland
Department of Justice Files 2007/50/130 and 2007/50/131, National
Archives of Ireland
The Laurence Griffin files, Garda Museum and Archives

TELEVISION DOCUMENTARIES

CSÍ – Cork's Bloody Secret, RTÉ One, broadcast 14 September 2009
CSÍ – The Missing Postman, RTÉ One, broadcast 5 October 2009

UNPUBLISHED MANUSCRIPTS

Ó Dúshláine, Tadhg, *Any News of Poor Larry?*
O'Mara, Harry, *Stradbally Case*

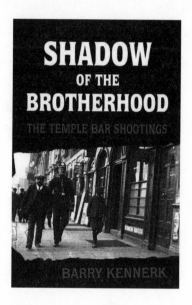

Shadow of the Brotherhood

Barry Kennerk

ISBN: 978 1 85635 677 0

In the early hours of Thursday 31 October 1867, Constable John Keena and Sergeant Stephen Kelly of the Dublin Metropolitan Police are shot in Temple Bar. Although surgeons are able to save Kelly's life, Keena succumbs to his wounds a few days later. Superintendent Daniel Ryan and his detective squad launch a massive manhunt.

It soon becomes clear that the assassin is a member of a radical republican shooting squad which sees policemen, informers and members of the judiciary as potential targets. In a race against time, the police must capture the gang before it strikes again.

www.mercierpress.ie

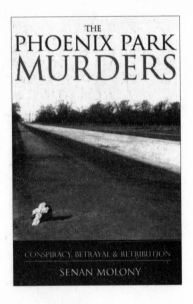

Also Available from Mercier Press

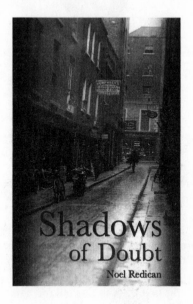

SHADOWS OF DOUBT

Noel Redican

ISBN: 978 1 85635 594 0

In 1928 Seán Harling, a Civic Guard and former republican, shot dead a known IRA member, Timothy Coughlan. Harling claimed he had been ambushed but, though cleared of wrong-doing by a tribunal and inquest, he was forced to give up his job and flee the country.

Revealing private conversations that suggest Harling was playing a much murkier role than even his detractors had suggested, Noel Redican delves into the dark and shifting history of Ireland's first decade as an independent state, when politics was fluid and murderous tensions were never far from the surface.

www.mercierpress.ie